# SPANIELS

After the Painting by Miss Maud Earl ]     [The Property of Mr. Arkwright.

**1899 IDEALS OF INTERNATIONAL GUNDOG LEAGUE SPORTING SPANIEL SOCIETY**

# SPANIELS:

## THEIR BREAKING FOR SPORT AND FIELD TRIALS.

BY

## H. W. CARLTON.

WITH AN INTRODUCTION BY

## W. ARKWRIGHT.

*Third (Revised) Edition.*

LONDON:

THE FIELD PRESS LTD.,

Windsor House, Bream's Buildings, E.C. 4.

1ST EDITION    ...  March, 1915.

2ND EDITION    ...  March, 1921.

3RD EDITION    ...  October, 1922.

# PREFACE TO FIRST EDITION

THE honour of holding the first Field Trials for Spaniels, in January, 1899, rests with the Sporting Spaniel Society. Their example has been followed to such purpose that during last season no less than eight spaniel field trial meetings were held. The hoped-for result has come to pass. Methods have been evolved by which a spaniel's effectiveness in the field, as a general purpose dog, has been increased and his work improved.

Despite this, no book dealing with the breaking of the spaniel on modern lines has been published during these fifteen years.

No apology for *a* book on spaniels is therefore necessary. The deficiencies of this particular book must be set down, by the charitable, to the fact that it is an attempt to break somewhat fresh ground. It is not suggested that the several methods herein indicated are the only or possibly the best means of teaching a spaniel

his many duties ; they have, however, all passed
the test of experience.

My warmest thanks are due to Mr. W.
Arkwright, of Sutton Scarsdale—to whose
initiative and support the spaniel as a gundog
owes so much—not only for his introduction,
but also for valuable suggestions on the subject-
matter of other parts of the book and his
permission to reproduce the picture in the
frontispiece.

*May*, 1914.

# PREFACE TO THIRD EDITION

THE demand for a third edition following so soon after the reprint of March, 1921, has emboldened me to take a further step along a way hitherto untrodden, and introduce an entirely fresh chapter upon the psychology of the dog as bearing upon dog-breaking in general. It skirts the eternal question " Do animals reason ? " and it seems that even if the dog is incapable of explaining the " Why" and "Wherefore" of its actions, this is no good reason why the breaker of the dog should be left in like case; it is hoped that the chapter may give the breaker some clues that up to now have been lacking.

Further than this, " dog sense " is generally held to be the attribute that specially distinguishes the good from the bad breaker, and has been set down as purely intuitive. Consisting, however—as it would appear mainly to do—of an appreciation of the working of the dog mind, it is hoped that this additional chapter may in some sort provide a substitute for intuition in the case of those who are lacking in it.

The original text has also been revised, and such additions made as the intervening years' experience and talks with fellow-breakers have suggested. The preliminary notes to Part I. have been entirely re-written, and now contain a short review of the various breeds of Spaniels from a working point of view. Some suggestions as to water-work have also been added to Chapter X.

Lubenham, Market Harborough.
*September,* 1922.

# CONTENTS.

# INTRODUCTION.

I AM highly pleased at having been asked to write an introduction to this book of Mr. Carlton's, because I consider it so thorough a book. But at the same time I am painfully aware that its very thoroughness creates my difficulty. What is there left to me to write about except the zeal and ability of the author—although a panegyric in this place would hardly give him pleasure, besides being not quite to the purpose?

To gain time for myself, I will draw attention to the rather obvious fact that Mr. Carlton's work fills a gap in gundog literature; for it is, I believe, the only one that has ever been devoted in its entirety to the breaking—to the education of the spaniel. Now this seems all the more remarkable since the spaniel is the most ancient of our gundogs, and is undoubtedly the one most generally useful to the sportsman—being able to understudy, on an emergency, all

the other members of the family, be they
pointers, setters, or retrievers, while none of
these can return the compliment.

In the past, therefore, it has been a reproach
to English sportsmen that there did not
exist an exhaustive treatise on the art of
spaniel-breaking; and it is certainly a feather
in the cap of the Author that he should be
the pioneer in dealing seriously with an important
subject. Again, not only does he busy himself
with the breaking of the dogs, but also (which is
far more important) he includes in his scope the
breaking of the would-be spaniel-breaker
himself! In short, that which has been done for
the other breeds by various writers in many
pamphlets, retrievers especially having a little
library to themselves, Mr. Carlton seems to have
succeeded in condensing into a single volume.
A condensation that ought to be peculiarly
seasonable in view of a newborn disposition of
the community to include among its pastimes,
along with its golf and its bridge, the personal
training of gundogs for public trials.

But stay! While I am extolling the universal
qualities of these spaniel-breaking essays, the
idea strikes me that perhaps they may not start
quite early enough in the spaniel's career. How

about choosing the puppy that is to share with one in the application of all these well-reasoned maxims? Will not this subject allow me to introduce a few theories of my own? I think so—even if I have to apologise for descending to rather homely levels.

Bearing in mind the French proverb that "*Bon chien chasse de Race*"—*i.e.*, the good dog comes from hunting stock — and also remembering that Frenchmen are masters of precept, much must depend on getting a likely pup to start with.

First, then, as to the pup's actual pedigree, he should have a first-rate dam : one that excels in natural talent—one, if possible, that is the favourite shooting-companion of her master. His sire's excellencies there is not quite so much necessity to investigate : for one reason, because the owner of a good bitch will almost certainly have exercised care in her mating.

Secondly, choose from the litter a puppy with a big, round skull, well filled over the temples, and a look of dauntless curiosity in his well-opened eyes. See that he does not run back from your inspection, to hide himself under the straw ; see that on being handled he does not make water, which is a sure sign of nerves morbidly developed. Nerves in excess are a nuisance, and are to be dreaded quite as much as a lazy and phlegmatic disposition.

And now a necessary word or two on the *Natural Qualities*, which are those qualities that the most capable master cannot put into his pupil, and without which no spaniel can become a first-rater. I will enumerate them here, so that they may be kept in mind right through the educational course:—

(1) *Docility*, which is the wish to learn—the desire to please his master.

(2) *Courage*, which makes a dog unconscious of fatigue—which will crash him through thorns, and brambles, and gorse—which will force him across a river in flood.

(3) *Nose*, which really stands for keenness of scenting power combined with the sense to apply it aright.

(4) *Style*, which is chiefly merry bustle, with flashing, quivering tail—and head ever alert, now high to reach a body-scent, now low to investigate a track : attributes that are most precious to a tired man or to one vexed at a bad shot. Style exhibits itself also in work of a decisive, dashing kind : for instance, in spring-

ing a rabbit with such vehemence as to frighten
it into leaving its covert post-haste.

The above are the purely natural qualities,
which I believe to be hereditary, which are
certainly impossible of inculcation by any
breaker.

There are, besides, two additional qualities
that are often *natural ;* but, if not natural, that
may be, to a certain extent, *acquired.*

(1) *Retrieving* is often inherent in a spaniel
puppy, and is exhibited by a partiality for lifting
anything that is handy and carrying it about.
Such a puppy usually has in addition a soft, dry
mouth, and he will make the best retriever of
all. But many good dogs require some
schooling in the retrieve, and this will vary in
degree — from ordinary cajoleries to the
desperate methods of the so-called *French
System.*

(2) *Water-work.*—Most spaniel puppies take
to this naturally, but not all of them. Some do
not by instinct know the way to swim, others do
not care for the shock of cold water. They can
one and all be taught by kind firmness and perseverance, but these artificially made swimmers
are never the *great* water dogs—with their cork-
like abilities of dealing with rock and surf and

whirlpool. It is probable that a remote strain of English Water-spaniel is responsible for the wonderful powers of some strains, and it is well to remember that a thick, wavy, oily coat usually goes with proficiency in swimming.

And now, for a few strokes having dipped my own oar into the water while calm, let me ship it again and resign in favour of a right skilful navigator, who can and will pilot anyone of sufficient eagerness to that country where is to be discovered the one priceless dog—the Perfect Spaniel.

WILLIAM ARKWRIGHT.

*May*, 1914.

# SPANIELS:

## Their Breaking for Sport and Field Trials.

## PART I.—PRELIMINARY.

THE suggestions contained in this book apply to the breaking of all land Spaniels, whether Springers, Cockers, Clumbers, Sussex or Field Spaniels, and of Water Spaniels when used for work on land. At Field Trials all the breeds are expected both to hunt and to retrieve, and whether running singly or in brace or team are judged on similar lines. In the early days of Field Trials retrieving was optional in stakes confined to Cockers, but at the present day the Cocker is expected to retrieve, although most judges would not ask it to try conclusions with a hare. So far, therefore, as Field Trials are concerned, the choice of a breed depends upon the fancy of the owner, though he can hardly expect the Cocker to compete on equal terms with his big brother the Springer.

So far as concerns the merits of any particular

B

breed for sport the matter is not quite so simple, and there are admirers of the less popular breeds who assert that the nature of the ground on which most Field Trials are run unduly favours the Springer. However this may be, it is quite possible that some shooting men may have found by experience that their district is more suitable for one breed than another. That this was so in the past, when facilities for travel were few and the Spaniels would only be used in their owners' own neighbourhood, there is certainly some evidence. The County of Sussex gives its name to one breed, and the Norfolk Spaniel (the precursor of the English Springer) would appear to take its name from the Duke and not from the County of Norfolk, and thus point to another connection with Sussex. The Clumber was for many years confined to the kennels of owners living in the neighbourhood of the estate from which its name is taken, and so may presumably have been specially adapted to the character of the ground in and around the Dukeries. The Cocker, according to the older writers, is so called on account of its "appropriation to wood-cock shooting," and, according to more recent writers, the Welsh and Devonshire strains were particularly adapted to the low and close-growing cover with which they would be called upon to deal.

The reader may justly complain that the above

notes are not very helpful ; truth to tell, my own experience does not point to any breed being specially adapted to any particular character of ground, though with regard to the Clumber I have found that it never goes so well as when hunting short standing bracken. I am also inclined to doubt whether a Cocker can work thick close cover better than a moderate-sized Springer, and this doubt is justified by the experience of a pre-eminent handler who used to work teams of both Cockers and Springers, and found that the latter, from their extra weight and leg drive, could get through cover the former could not negotiate. It must be remembered that a keen active Spaniel does not attempt to get through low-growing cover standing up, and that consequently the height of the dog is not so important a factor as at first blush would appear to be the case.

There are good and bad strains and good and bad specimens of every breed, but I think that none will gainsay the general conclusions that the Clumber is the easiest of all to break, and that the Springer is probably the most difficult; that, although in the early days of Field Trials a Clumber carried all before her, the Clumber of show-bench type and the old-fashioned Field are too ponderous and slow and easily tire ; that as between the Springer and the Cocker of Field Trial strain there is little to choose, except as to size; that the Irish Water Spaniel is too large for many of the purposes for which a land Spaniel is required. A Sussex I have never owned, but from what I have seen I fancy they are apt to carry too low a head, and thus be inclined to run live foot scents and so miss rabbits in their seats—but it may have been the breakers and not the dogs that were to blame.

# CHAPTER I.

## GENERAL PRINCIPLES.

THE first maxim that every would-be successful breaker must accept is that the word "breaking" as applied to dogs is merely a figure of speech. I should not be far wrong in saying that it is impossible for a "broken"—in anything approaching the literal meaning of the word—dog to be a first-class one. "Training" even is perhaps too harsh a word to apply to a process that consists of an easily graduated series of lessons given without a trace of asperity—at any rate, at first.

The second maxim is of equal importance. It is insisted on by W. Arkwright in a few all too short notes on spaniel breaking in "British Dogs" in the words "The preliminary course is by far the most important."

Unless the breaker has these two maxims indelibly inscribed upon his heart, he can never hope for any consistent measure of success. They are without doubt the keynote of all good breaking ; without them it is impossible to get the most out of a spaniel in the field or —which is the same thing in a higher degree—

to hope for any success at field trials. Whatever
may be written in the public Press to the contrary—generally either in ignorance of field trial
work or from the acerbity engendered by non-
success—work at field trials is only work in the
field brought to a state more nearly bordering
on perfection, with spaniels possessing exceptional natural ability; but more of this in the
last chapter.

To break for sport and to break for field trials
are one and the same thing, and there is nothing
mystic or occult about either of them.  Given
natural ability, perfect work depends upon the
perfection of the preliminary course—generally
termed "handbreaking"—and the application
of this perfection to work in the field.  It is as
reasonable to expect perfect work in a spaniel
whose handbreaking has been neglected as it
would be to expect a child to read before he has
learned his alphabet.  The work of our best field
trial spaniels appears to those who see it for the
first time nothing short of a marvel; yet it is
but the climax of a carefully graduated series of
lessons, each lesson repeated until it becomes
second nature, and even when thoroughly learned
repeated again and again, lest its impression fade.

Spaniel breaking must therefore proceed on
the following general lines:

1st.—You must teach your spaniel what you
want him to do.

2nd.—You must see that he does it at times when there is no strong counter-attraction.

3rd.—You must see that he does it at times when he particularly wants to do something else—*e.g.*, chase a rabbit that is moving off in front of him. In other words, you must make him carry out—as it were in dumb show—the actions you want him to reproduce when it comes to real business.

The lessons of the first and second class merge into one another and constitute handbreaking. They consist in teaching the dog that certain words and signs on your part must be followed at all times—in the end instantaneously—by certain acts on his. To achieve this it is absolutely necessary that each word or sign should have one meaning to the dog, and one only. To say " down," when you want your dog to drop and also when you want to stop him jumping up on you, can only create confusion in his mind and retard his progress. It is also necessary that you should never give the word or sign without seeing to it that the appropriate act follows. It will not do if the act follows sometimes, it must do so always—without exception. Every time a command is given and compliance does not follow or is not enforced, you will have lost ground. Not only will the habit of obedience be weakened, but the impression on the dog's mind of the meaning of the command will have become les deep.

Do not let the above lead you to the conclusion that your dog is to become a mere automaton. " Brains " are a valuable attribute in any gundog. Good breaking should develop his intelligence as well as control his actions.

It should not be necessary to point out that, until their meanings are taught, your words convey nothing to your dog. It is, however, no rare thing to see a puppy punished for not obeying a command that must be to him but empty sound.

Remember always that your dog's outlook upon life is not so precise and clear cut as your own, and that in everything you teach him in the early days it is up to you to make the subject-matter of your lessons stand out clearly and with certainty from the mists of his mind. It is unfair, both to your puppy and your efforts to train him, to endow him with a mental equipment equal to your own. With this necessity for clarity and certainty in mind, do not use his name with varying inflections of voice as a substitute for definite words of command.

Never punish your dog for disobedience until you are sure that he not only understands the meaning of your command, but also knows that it is incumbent upon him to obey it—not merely optional. If you are uncertain of this, give the dog the benefit of the doubt.   Instead of punishment, take immediate steps to impress upon him your meaning and see that he complies.

Thrashing is not, as so many thoughtless breakers seem to think, a means of education in itself; the correct place it should take in breaking is discussed in Chapter XI.

To quote Arkwright once again: "To a spaniel's character incessant thrashings are fatal, as under such treatment he becomes either cowed or case-hardened, according to his individual temperament, but never broken." Doubly true is this if the thrashings are undeserved.   Under just treatment he will render you the hero-worship of a "dame's school" boy to his Eton brother; you will be to him the one whom it is his pleasure to serve and to whom he instinctively looks for guidance if he finds himself at fault.

See as much of your dog as you possibly can. Gain his confidence—you will do no good with a dog that is suspicious of you.   Give yourself a chance of discovering any outstanding traits in his character and apply the knowledge so gained in your treatment of him—it is rarely that any two dogs can be broken in exactly the same way.

Leave no stone unturned to get a good performance as the wind-up of every lesson time.

Refrain from continuously nagging at your

dog; assume that he desires to please you and in consequence is wishful of obeying your commands; do not pick a quarrel with him needlessly, but seek to keep on good terms as long as you possibly can.

Do not expect your breaking to result in even progress; it is sure to have its ups and downs.

One day all will go well, the next your puppy can do nothing right. He has his good days and his bad, but so have you. Your humours act and re-act on one another. On his bad days blame yourself, get him to perform well some easier task, and take him home.

Just as there are bad days, so there are bad places, which your puppy peoples for himself with a host of malignant genii. Associations are strong. If your puppy has once been specially perverse, avoid the scene of his perverseness and never give him a lesson there again.

Never give a lesson unless you have your puppy's whole attention, or continue one when you have lost it. To do so is to annoy both him and yourself and profit neither.

Take every opportunity of getting him interested in the scent of game; you cannot directly teach him to use his nose, but you can, and must, give him opportunities to teach himself.

Take every opportunity of developing his brains. Let him find out things for himself where possible. Do not be impatient if, on his first experience of the road, he jibs at every cow and smells at every passer-by. The world is new to him, and he must get to know it in his own way—mostly by his nose. Have you ever noticed how throughout his life a dog relies on nose? He will pick you out in a crowd by sight, but rarely seems sure that you are you until he has your scent.

For successful breaking patience is more than a virtue—it is an essential.

In many of the older books you are advised to break your puppy by taking him out with a broken dog. In later books this method is derided. The derision has, I think, been overdone. There is a happy medium. To let the example of a broken spaniel be your sole method is obviously wrong—as likely as not you would find your puppy waiting outside a thick place for the older dog to put the rabbits out to him. Breaking by jealousy—especially in retrieving —is, however, bulking large in the eyes of many modern gundog men.

It is impossible to lay down any rules for applying it, and the subject is not dealt with explicitly hereafter. Your own " dog sense " can be your only guide. Perhaps a single instance out of my own experience may be of use. A

puppy—nearly finished—was perfect at retrieving
rabbits cold, but refused to pick them up when
freshly killed. At each refusal I tied him up,
went home and brought another dog, and sent
this latter to retrieve. On replacing the rabbit,
the culprit each time did all that had before been
asked of him in vain. As a finish I used him as
a retriever a time or two while another dog was
hunting. By these methods—both based on
jealousy—his fault was cured.

When you give a command or signal to your
dog, do it with your whole heart. The flabbier
your state of mind, the flabbier is your dog's
response. The intangible bond between man
and dog varies much with various dogs and
varies more with various men. A harsh and
inconsistent breaker can rarely exert, or a cowed
or case-hardened dog be susceptible to, this
power of will. That it forms an important
element in good breaking I am convinced.

Avoid the use of lead and check-cord so far
as possible. Your puppy will progress more
rapidly without them.

Finally—again in Arkwright's words—" To
train a dog properly a man must be always
attentively on the watch to nip crime in the bud;
and it is the want of this faculty in would-be
breakers that is accountable for so many failures,
while the possessors of it are succeeding without
apparent trouble or even method." I have in

the following notes endeavoured to suggest a method ; the development of this faculty rests with you.   Its foundations lie in the interest you take in the progress of your breaking, and it is built up by observance of the rule, "Watch your dog."

# CHAPTER II.

## THE PERFECT SPANIEL.

"THE preliminary course is by far the most important"—it is impossible to repeat this too often. But on what lines should it run? To what is it preliminary?

Before starting to break your spaniel, you must have—and keep—clearly before you what you want him to do when broken.

Everyone who uses a spaniel as a general purpose dog knows that he wants it—

(1) To find the stuff.

(2) Not to spoil the shot.

(3) To retrieve—when required.

This statement of the case is in absurdly simple terms. It serves, however, as affording three headings under which to consider the matter more in detail, viz., hunting, steadiness, and retrieving.

### 1.—HUNTING.

*Method, Pace, and Style.*—It is not enough that your spaniel should find some stuff—he should find all the stuff within easy gunshot on either side of you.

In the eyes of field trial judges there is no fault—except a hard mouth—that is so unforgivable as passing stuff, and the commission of this fault is, I think, more often due to want of thoroughness in working the ground than to lack of nose. The fault that is hardly less—perhaps equally —unforgivable is pottering.

To the man who goes out "spanieling" for his own amusement, I fancy that pottering annoys him more than passing stuff—the pottering is a visible source of annoyance all the time, whereas the stuff his dog has missed might, for all he knows, not be there at all. Personally—and I am not alone in this—I would rather shoot over a dog that goes a good pace and misses a rabbit every now and then than one that goes but half the pace and finds every one. It is to my mind a more artistic and enjoyable performance, and—noses being equal —the fast dog's bag will be the larger at the end of the day; he will have covered much more ground.

Whatever views you may hold as to passing stuff, it is undeniable that the two great things to aim at in your breaking are an effective method of working the ground and pace—so long as the dog does not over-run his nose.

Style, also, is by no means a negligible quality. It is the outward manifestation of keenness and game-finding capacity. It may be spoilt by bad breaking; it may be developed as a consequence of the development of the faculties of which it is the index ; but it cannot, I think, be put into a dog that is wholly lacking in it. Some naturally fast puppies are apt, in their early days, to gallop their ground from the mere joy of pace; when steadied down their style improves—their pace becomes subservient to their nose.

Method of working and pace are matters directly within the control of the breaker—the one absolutely, the other in a minor degree.

A spaniel is often the counterpart of his handler; if the handler is dull and listless, and especially if he takes a somewhat tepid interest in his dog, his dog is slow and apathetic. If the handler is keen and alert to discover the least indication that his dog is on a scent, the dog responds to his handler's interest and hunts the better for him.

Method of working is a bigger matter. It must of course depend to a large extent upon the nature of the ground. Nothing need be said here as to working a large isolated patch of brambles, gorse, or briars, or a hedgerow. A spaniel that will not work the thick is no spaniel at all.

On open ground, such as a rough piece or an expanse of dead bracken or heather, it is no uncommon sight to see a spaniel working out of gunshot more often than within.

If there has been some pretence of breaking he may trot off listlessly straight in front of the gun, feel that he has got far enough, wait for his handler to come up to him, and then trot on again. He may start a rabbit or two in the course of the day—the gun would probably have kicked up most of them himself. It may be that when at the limit of his range he may flush a pheasant ; the gun would have had a better chance if the flushing had been left to him. Gun and dog together are beating a strip of country not much more than 5yds. wide.

In neither of these cases does the dog add much to the bag ; he might almost as well have been left at home, or, if a good retriever, have been used solely as such.

To be a really effective aid to sport, the spaniel should be working a strip—with the gun walking up the centre of it—30yds. or 40yds. wide, now going out and working to the right, turning smartly, crossing in front of the gun and going out an equal distance to the left, turning again and crossing—quartering his ground—not dwelling on a rabbit run or other such unprofitable scent, bringing every tussock and bush within the range of his nose, pushing through every patch that is not fully commanded by it from outside—all the time with tail going merrily and every action instinct with the joy of hunting and a keen desire to get the gun a shot.

I must not be taken to mean that the quartering should be unduly systematic or is all that
is required.   Mere quartering is to reduce the
spaniel to the level of a beater.   He must be
using his nose every moment of the time, taking
every advantage of the wind and working every
likely bit of ground—all the time with half an
eye on his handler's whereabouts.

With a spaniel hunting as I suggest he should,
it is obvious that pace is greatly to be desired.
He has to work—and work thoroughly—to and
fro across a strip not less than 30yds. wide,
while the gun is walking up the middle of it.   If
he is slow, time will be cut to waste ; or possibly
the gun may get impatient, hurry the dog, and
make him miss much ground.   In either case the
bag suffers ; and the best dog is the dog that
best fills the bag.

In connection with pointers and setters it has
frequently been stated that pace and nose are by
no means canine opposites ; with spaniels, this
is equally true.   Pace as a rule is associated
with keeness, and for this reason, the fast dog
is more likely to be using his nose than a slower
one.   The keener the dog, the more likely he is
to bring into play every game-finding attribute
he has ; of these he is well aware that his nose
is the best and most reliable.

*Standing Rabbits.*—Suppose your spaniel is
working in the open and finds a rabbit in its

seat, what is ne to do? Most spaniel men aie agreed that he should not catch it, and that, if he does, he should either drop it on command or bring it to hand. Should the dog poke the rabbit up at once or should he set ("stand") it? If he finds well within gunshot, it does not matter which he does. It is possible, however, that when at the limit of his proper range, especially on a cross wind, he may have got the scent of the rabbit some distance off. If he pokes it up at once, the shot will be lost, whereas if he stands it, the gun will have time to get up. One can hardly expect the average spaniel to make fine distinctions as to distance, especially when he is drawing up on a scent. It is therefore better to teach him, if you can, to stand his rabbits in all cases, and to start them only when the gun comes up or on command.

I do not mean that he should need advancing like a pointer or setter or should stand indefinitely. As to the two extremes, I think it better that he should dash in and poke the rabbit up at once than stand too long. The latter not only wastes time but is apt to develop into standing empty seats.

As to this matter of standing rabbits, it may be remarked that in the Field Trial Regulations of the International Gundog League Sporting Spaniel Society—the pioneer of spaniel field

trials—it is described as " an additional excellence." Although this is so, there are members
—and those not the least notable—of that society
who have even yet not quite made up their minds
upon the subject.

It will be noted that the above remarks as to
standing rabbits are confined to open ground.
If a spaniel is working thick cover, such as gorse,
he should at once put up anything he finds and
hustle it until it breaks cover and gives the gun
a shot. It is wonderful how adept a good dog
gets at putting out rabbits to the gun and dropping—even without a shot being fired—as soon
as he sees that they are well away in the open.

*Stamina and Perseverance.*—In addition,
your spaniel should be able to keep going all
day at his best pace—a matter of stamina,
courage, and condition ; he should also keep on
hunting, though he finds no stuff. Both these
qualities are of great importance on most rough
shoots, and it is much to be deplored that they
can rarely be tested at field trials, the one for
lack of time, the other because there must be
a quantity of stuff if many spaniels are to have
a trial in the course of a short November day.

## 2.—STEADINESS.

The only degree of steadiness that is essential
is such as will ensure that the dog does not spoil
the shot and will not, by retrieving without

orders, put up other stuff out of shot or while the gun is unloaded.

The best way to compass this is to break your dog to drop to fur and wing and also drop to shot.

It is, of course, equally good if the dog, instead of dropping, halts. Dropping is, however, the more easily learned ; to stop motion is more difficult than to change its direction. Moreover, a dropped dog has to get up before he runs in, and so is one degree further removed from unsteadiness than if he only halts. It is better that the dropping should take the form of sitting on his haunches than lying at full length. Although the latter position is yet another degree removed from running in, it precludes " marking," a most important faculty in all dogs that retrieve.

Many seasoned dogs, when working in cover over which they cannot see when sitting, acquire the habit of standing up on their hind legs to get a better view. This is undoubtedly the best position of all, but I have never heard of any spaniel being directly broken to do this. It comes from keenness and is not taught; I see no reason why it should not be—if life were long enough.

In connection with steadiness, as with hunting, there are two matters for which a spaniel is not usually tried at field trials. The one is

walking to heel; the other steadiness in a grouse
butt or at a partridge drive or covert shoot.
Despite this, no spaniel can be called a perfect
one unless he can act in these respects as well
as a no-slip retriever.

### 3.—RETRIEVING.

Your spaniel having dropped to fur or wing
should not, of course, go in to retrieve without
orders. He should not even start forward at
the shot.

In the case, too, of fur or feather which he has
not found or even seen, he should be broken to
drop instantly to shot at whatever pace he may
be going.

Having dropped, he should not move until he
is sent out to retrieve or has got the command
to go on hunting, the usual word for which is
" Gone away."

With regard to retrieving fur which your
spaniel has not found, or feather, a spaniel's
duties do not differ from a retriever's. When,
however, it comes to retrieving fur which he has
found, a complication arises.

Suppose a rabbit which your spaniel has
started from its seat goes 20yds.—all out of
his sight—is then shot at and legged, and
crawls on another 30yds., your spaniel should
get on the line at or just beyond the seat

and take it from there right up to the rabbit. This line is for its first 20yds. a live foot scent, and it is only for the last 30yds. that it is what is generally termed a blood-scent. When your spaniel is hunting he should not—as pointed out in the first section of this chapter— take any notice of a live foot-scent unless his nose tells him that the rabbit is just ahead of him, or at most should just acknowledge it and leave it.

A retriever is broken to disregard a live scent at all times and under all circumstances; he is kept to heel unless the stuff is down. Not so the poor spaniel. He finds a rabbit in its seat, starts it, sees it no more, but hears the shot; if the rabbit is hit, he will be expected, on receiving the appropriate command, to take the line from seat to rabbit; if it is missed he must be prepared, on receiving the " Gone away," to ignore the same line absolutely and go on hunting as if it did not exist.

To unravel this complication in your spaniel's mind takes more time than any of the spectators, possibly even some of the judges, at field trials can appreciate—unless they are themselves breakers.

The safest way is to break your spaniel to disregard foot-scents at all times except when he receives some such command as " Fetch it." As a rule, and especially at field trials—where the rabbits may have been stunk out for weeks, and are possibly on the move all day—there will be many live foot-scents that your spaniel should ignore to each one that he should take. Let ignoring them be the rule; let taking them—which is the exception—be the subject of a special word of command.

This complication apart, all that is expected of a retriever is expected of a spaniel. He should "mark" well, cast himself, work to hand if necessary, take the wind, be fast and sure on a line, pick up smartly, be tender mouthed, return at the gallop, and deliver well to hand.

All this the field trial spaniel of to-day does as well as—some think better than—the retriever. In addition, he does all the other things a retriever is not usually asked to do.

# PART II.—HANDBREAKING.

## CHAPTER III.

### EARLY PUPPYHOOD LESSONS.

IN most books on dog-breaking the reader is advised to spend his time during the early months of the puppy's life—say for the first four months after weaning—in making the puppy " generally obedient."

This is no doubt most excellent advice. The difficulty is as to the lines on which the breaker should proceed, and as to the nature of the lessons best adapted to secure general obedience. One should no doubt teach the puppy his name, which may be done by calling his name and patting him or giving him a piece of biscuit. One should also, no doubt, make the puppy gallop up to one on his name being called— which may be done in much the same way. And one should make him go to his kennel when desired. This presents more difficulty. Person-ally, if a puppy is recalcitrant in this respect,

I generally get him to me, and either pick him up and carry him in or put on him a collar with a short light cord attached and make him comply by an admixture of cajolery and gentle force, and end up with a reward.

In these lessons, as with all other lessons during early puppyhood, the four cardinal principles are :—

(1) Never give an order without seeing that the puppy complies with it; he has got to learn to obey you always, not sometimes.

(2) Always be absolutely gentle, both in voice and action—when you come to work in the field, you want a bold, keen dog, not a cowed and listless wreck.

(3) Never give an order with which you cannot secure compliance without a display of harshness.

(4) Never persist in any lesson which is becoming a bore to the puppy.

The nearer these earliest lessons can be approximated to a game, in the puppy's eyes, the better.

Within the limits laid down above, the ingenious breaker may teach these lessons in any way that occurs to him, or give such other lessons with the object of inculcating general obedience as his ingenuity may suggest.

But why, in these early days, should one

confine one's lessons to securing *general* obedience? Why not begin now in teaching and securing obedience in some of the *particular* matters which you will eventually have to teach your dog?

In the last chapter a spaniel's work has been considered under the three heads of hunting, steadiness, and retrieving. Although this is the natural order in which a spaniel's duties are performed, it is not the order in which his preliminary education should be conducted. A spaniel's first lessons should, as a rule, be taken in hand in the reverse order, *i.e.*, retrieving, steadiness, and, lastly, hunting; and this reversal is greatly accentuated in the case of a puppy under six months old. I do not mean that you should keep your puppies carefully secluded in kennel or run at such times as they are not being given definite lessons. Give them as much liberty and see as much of them as you can. They must get to know their world and learn to put implicit confidence in you. Seize every opportunity of getting scent into their noses. Personally, as soon as my puppies can walk I spend many an odd few minutes with them among the adjacent rabbit burrows and runs, and watch for the first indication of their taking up a scent. Avoid, however, places where, as the puppies grow older, they are likely to get a " view " and chase; take care also that

they do not acquire too great a predilection for
runs ; in both cases prevention is better than
cure.

One of the methods of teaching retrieving
(other methods are mentioned in Chapter IV.)
is to throw something for the dog to fetch,
and, without the use of a check-cord or other
artificial aid, induce the dog to bring the object
up to you.   This method can be no less—in my
opinion more—successfully employed when the
dog is well under the age of six months than at
any later age.

The other lesson which can be successfully
taught during these early days is dropping to
command and to hand, which, as extended to fur,
feather, and shot, is, as I hope the reader will have
gathered from Chapter II., the foundation of
steadiness.

This "dropping" is not only valuable as
being one of the things that your dog will
eventually have to learn; it has also a value
peculiar to itself in inculcating general obedience
and making the dog feel himself subservient to
his master ; it is, in fact, of the very essence of
all good spaniel breaking.   A spaniel that will
drop instantly to command or hand, wherever he
may be and at whatever pace he may be going,
has proceeded further in his breaking and
approached more nearly to the completely
broken dog than the performance of such an

apparently simple action would lead the novice to believe.

But I can hear some of my field trial friends mutter the ominous word "overbreaking," and can also hear some of them advocate letting your puppy run wild and chase, if opportunity offers, up to the age of as much as twelve months. If the would-be breaker is hasty in temper, impatient, and harsh of tongue, I should advise him to give heed to their muttering and postpone the dropping lessons until a later age; or, better still, give up all idea of trying to break the puppy himself. If, however, he lays to heart and carries out in their entirety the general principles laid down above—and in particular that as to gentleness—he need have no fear; his puppy will be as keen and full of dash at the end of these earliest lessons as the puppy that has run riot during their period; indeed, it is more than likely that if the riotous puppy is at all a nervous one, the sudden check he will have to receive may break his spirit; the gentle insistence on the graduated series of lessons here advised can never do so.

The younger the dog, the more plastic is his mind, and the fewer are the bad habits which he will have contracted, and which the breaker may have to cast out with check-cord and with chastisement.

A dog, too, that is fit to shoot over at ten

months old—a dog of mine, broken from earliest
puppyhood on the lines here suggested, was a
prize-winner in an important field trial stake
under that age—puts on an extra six months
to his life of usefulness.

## RETRIEVING.

As soon, then, after your puppy is weaned as
you feel that, by judicious gifts of biscuit from
your hand and other endearing arts, you have
gained his confidence, take your heart in your
hand and begin your lessons in retrieving. Be
sure, however, that your puppy's confidence in
you is thoroughly established; it is not enough
that he should not fight shy of you; he must be
eager to get to you whenever you appear in
sight. It is unreasonable to expect him to bring
to you what you have thrown for him to fetch if
he will not race up to you without this counter
attraction in his mouth. With these retrieving
lessons in view, it is useful to get him to associate
some such signal as clapping your hands with
his race up to you.

The first actual lesson in retrieving is for you
an anxious moment, for if your puppy resolutely
refuses to pick up what you have thrown for
him, your lessons—so far as retrieving is concerned—will have to be postponed until a later
day in his career, and you will have lost much of

the pleasure that is to be derived from the
awakening and improvement of his faculties and
the development of the personal bond between
yourself and him.

Two questions naturally arise : What are you
to throw for him to fetch, and where are you to
throw it ? Whatever you throw should be
thrown on grass, and not on gravel or anything
else that is likely to hurt his nose or mouth or
otherwise be unpleasant to him. So long as the
puppy can see to the ground the thing you
throw, a grass field is better than a close-shaven
lawn ; it is somewhat easier for the puppy to
pick up from it. A writer of authority on the
breaking of retrievers advocates taking the
puppy some fields away from home. Personally,
I have not found it necessary to go farther away
than the paddock adjoining the puppy's usual run.

Wherever the first lesson is given, it must be
in a place that is not the puppy's usual play-
ground, a place that is free from scent of rabbits
or game—which might prove too strong a
counter-attraction—and a place where there are
no distracting influences, such as other dogs, or
people, cattle, horses, or sheep, or noise of traffic.
This sounds like making a mountain out of a
molehill ; truly it is in itself a little thing, but
dog-breaking is a congeries of little things, and
it is of the utmost importance to make a good
start.

Whatever spot you fix upon, go there alone
with your puppy, and make much of him. By
and by take your pocket-handkerchief, knot
and re-knot it into a ball so that there are no
loose ends, get your puppy's interest in it
aroused, seize a moment when the puppy is
following hand and handkerchief in a forward
direction, and throw the handkerchief—of course
underhand and in continuation of the movement
the puppy is following—to a distance of a yard
or two, at the same time telling the puppy to
"Fetch" it. The puppy sees the handkerchief
go—as it were, "follows your hand"—and
gallops out after it and, we hope, picks it up.
If you now act as you have acted before, the
puppy is almost sure—for the first few lessons
at any rate—to race up to you with the handkerchief just as he had done before without it.
Whenever he hesitates run away from him and he
will probably follow. If he starts towards you but
is shy of coming right up, try the effect of sitting
down. Be careful to avoid any sudden movement or snatching of the handkerchief—this will
make the puppy either sheer off from you or
drop the object; your aim is to get the object
straight from the puppy's mouth into your hand.
If by chance the puppy should be disinclined to
give up the object, you must not, of course,
engage in a tug-of-war with him, but must gently
open his mouth—if necessary, even putting your

hand in—and take the object from him. At all
hazards a hard mouth must be avoided, and a
tug-of-war is just the thing to give him one.

Whether it is better to reward the puppy with
a piece of biscuit or other dainty, or simply make
much of him, is a moot point; in these early
days a reward that appeals to his appetite is the
more acceptable, and makes the puppy keener to
come back to you ; on the other hand, if the
reward is given every time, the puppy is apt to
get into the habit of dropping the object in
expectation of the reward, a habit that is most
difficult to counteract and will cause you infinite
trouble in the future. A middle course is probably
the safer; give such a reward the first two or
three times, gradually cease doing so, and
reserve it for such time—which is almost sure
to arrive—as the puppy begins to show a
disinclination to return to you.

If the spot you fix on for these first lessons is
near the puppy's kennel, make a point of throwing the handkerchief away from the kennel and
intercepting him on his way to it ; the puppy's
inclination is, as a rule, to take his prize to, not
away from his kennel, and you can make this
inclination subservient to your own purpose. It
is cajolery and not forcefulness that in these
early lessons will win the day, and with it your
puppy's heart.

If by chance, when you have thrown the

handkerchief, the puppy does not go after it, but still has his attention attracted by your hand, do not try to make the puppy pick it up, but go and pick it up yourself, come back to the place from which you threw it, and try again. The reason the puppy did not go out is probably that he did not see the handkerchief leave your hand, and in these first lessons to take the puppy up to it and try to make him pick it up is only looking for trouble.

What you are to do if the puppy goes out but does not pick up the handkerchief is dealt with on the next page.

As to the nature of the edible reward, anything that the puppy likes and that is easily and cleanly carried in the pocket will do. Personally, I find small biscuits such as Ovals or Melox Marvels convenient for the pocket, and acceptable to the puppy. Small pieces of fried or boiled liver, or of cheese, have been recommended by various writers on retriever breaking, and may be usefully held in reserve for such time as the puppy's interest in biscuit may have waned.

Whatever form your edible reward may take, do not allow the puppy to snatch it from you; for this reason do not dangle it before his eyes, but put it unhesitatingly straight into his mouth. If ever during his later lessons he seems inclined to snatch, close your hand over it, say "Gently," and do not let him have it until he has got his eagerness under some measure of control. His proper understanding of "Gently" will be of great use to you in the future if he ever displays a tendency towards roughness in his retrieving work.

The use of the knotted handkerchief in these earliest lessons is a time-honoured institution. It is always handy, is soft, and easily attracts the puppy's attention. It may be also that it is of value as being such an intimate belonging of the breaker, and thus laying the foundation of the personal bond between him and his dog. Apart from this, anything soft and conspicuous will do.

If the puppy goes out after your handkerchief and refuses to pick it up, do not bother him further that day. Ring the changes upon change of schoolroom and change of object thrown, *e.g.*, rolled up rabbit skin, hat pad, tobacco pouch, glove stuffed with corks, etc., not risking more than one failure in any one day, until you have either discovered some scene and object with which you have achieved success or have exhausted your resources. If the latter, put off the puppy's retrieving education until such time as he is old enough for you to apply one or other of the methods indicated in Chapter IV. If you are successful in discovering a suitable school-room and a suitable object, proceed there and with that object in the same way as if success had crowned your first attempts.

Be careful not to overdo these retrieving lessons, or the puppy will cease to take an interest in them. Once a day, or at most twice a day—the second time after a good interval—is quite enough.

As the puppy grows, substitute for the knotted handkerchief other objects of gradually increasing bulk and weight. Personally, I abandon the handkerchief after the first week or so, and substitute a large leather glove filled with wine-bottle corks or a rolled up rabbit skin, according to the taste of the puppy, then a roll of house flannel or other similar material about a foot long, gradually enlarging its bulk and weighting it with a small sandbag, and finish up the hand-breaking with a roll made up to about the weight of a three-quarters-grown rabbit, and with a rabbit skin tied tightly over it with string in such a way as to leave no loose edges.

You have been advised to begin these lessons by throwing the object so that the puppy can see it on the ground. At as early a date in the puppy's education as possible you must alter this and throw the object into places where the puppy has to use his nose to find it, but where it is not too difficult for him to pick it up.

A most useful variation—possibly a substitute for all but the very first of these lessons—is to get the puppy to come upon the object without his having seen you throw it at all.   Walk with your puppy down wind, seize an opportunity when he is not looking, and drop or throw the object.   After a score of yards or so turn round, walk up wind towards the object, and encourage the puppy to hunt; if he has a nose and has had sufficient acquaintance with the object to recognise its scent, he should draw up to it from several yards.   As soon as he has hold of the object, act in the same way as you are advised to do when the puppy has seen the object thrown.

As soon, moreover, as your continued use of the " Fetch it " has led your puppy to connect this word with going out to retrieve, you should begin to teach him the word—*e.g.*, " Hie lost "—which you intend to use when sending him out to find something he has not seen fall.   A judicious mingling of the word he knows with the one you are teaching him, and your gradually working him up to the object he has not seen leave your hand—with frequent iterations of the new word—will soon teach him its meaning.   It should not be long before a single " Hie lost " will send your puppy out seeking for the object with all his soul ; but at first let the lesson be an easy one.

By this time the puppy should be quite proficient in bringing the bundle right up and

delivering it to hand without your being under the
necessity of running away from him. Be careful,
however, about facing the puppy as he comes in;
if he shows any inclination to drop the bundle
before it reaches your hand, keep your back
turned to him, and do not take it until he has got
well up to or even just past you. Be careful,
also, always to take the bundle from underneath
his jaws, pressing it upwards and towards his
mouth. If you take it from above or snatch it
from him, he will be apt to hang his head and
put the bundle down—a fault that you must
endeavour at all costs to avoid.

### Dropping to Command and Hand.

So far I have said nothing about dropping to
command or hand; but this must not be taken to
mean that lessons in this should be postponed
until the handbreaking in retrieving is finished
or even nearing its end. It is possibly advisable
to postpone such lessons until the end of the
first week or so of the retrieving lessons, but no
good purpose will be served by putting them off
longer.

There will be numerous occasions on which
you will be going to have a look at your puppies
in their enclosure. On these occasions arm
yourself with your usual " reward," and have
the puppies out one at a time. Seize a favour-

able opportunity, gently press down the puppy's hindquarters with one hand, and at the same time give him your reward with the other.  This should be accompanied with the word that you intend to use in future to drop your dog.

Most spaniel handlers, when their dog is hunting, drop him by the word " Up," generally and more easily pronounced " Hup."  The word is sharp and decisive, and, unless the breaker has a strong preference for some other, might as well be used.

As, then, you press down the hindquarters and give the reward, say " Up."  Do not at first try to prevent the puppy from getting up as soon as he likes.  All you are aiming at for the moment is to connect the " Up " with dropping, and the dropping with the gift of the reward. This will be the more easily accomplished if, after you have given the first lesson, you never give your puppy anything edible from your hand unless he is in the position of the drop.

In giving the first lessons to very young puppies you will find your task easier if you sit down on the ground and make the puppy drop by your side.

After the first few lessons make your puppy wait a second or two for the reward—if necessary, holding him down with your hand— and gradually increase the period of waiting and utilise the delay in holding up your dis-

engaged hand; carry this further by keeping
the puppy dropped a second or two—gradually
increasing the time—after you have given him
his reward, and do not let him get up until you
have given him the appropriate command.

As to what this should be, you will of course
bear in mind the future work of your puppy in
the field. In actual work he will have dropped
either to fur or feather or to shot; if he is
wanted to retrieve, you have already taught or
are in course of teaching him the appropriate
word; if he is not wanted to retrieve, he will
have to go on hunting, and the word usually
employed is " Gone away "; this word, then,
you had better use when allowing your puppy to
leave his drop.

So far, you have always kept near the puppy,
and have not attempted to keep him down long.
As soon as the puppy drops readily to the
combined influence of your " Up," and raised hand,
back a foot or two from him, with hand raised,
before giving the reward, and if he attempts to
get up and ignores your " Up," go back to him
and put him down again. Gradually increase
the distance you back from him, gradually omit
the upraising of the hand and reserve it for such
times as he attempts to get up, and every now
and then turn your back on him.

Never, on any pretext whatever, give him the
reward unless he has stayed dropped, exactly

where you put him, until you come back to him;
if he gets up while you are away from him, go
back and put him down in the exact place in
which he ought to have stayed, and retreat to
at least your original distance, before you come
back and reward him. Insistence on this exact-
ness will save you great trouble in the future,
and the puppy will soon understand that, until
he does exactly as you desire, he does not get
his reward.

In order to test whether the puppy has moved,
you will find it useful to make a mark on the
ground with your foot òr drop him close to some
mark on, or feature of, the ground that you can
readily bear in mind.

So far, the puppy has only dropped at your
side. As soon as he does this readily and stays
where he is put until he has got his reward and
received the " Gone away," you must one day
catch his eye when he is a yard or so away from
you, and hold up your hand—fortifying this if
necessary with your " Up " ; if he drops, do not at
first keep him waiting long, but go up to him and
give him his reward and the usual command; if he
does not drop you must gently force him to drop
in the exact place in which he ought to have done
so—if necessary, gently taking him to the spot—
retreat again, and keep him waiting for his
reward longer than you would have done if he
had dropped to your original command. He

will soon tumble to the fact that the more readily
he drops, the sooner he will get his reward.

As the puppy gets proficient at dropping a
yard or so from you, gradually increase the
distance until he finally drops readily and smartly
to hand or command, however far from you he
may be.

In all these lessons be careful to proceed
slowly, insist on an exact compliance, increase
the difficulty of them gradually, and if you feel
that you are going too fast for the puppy, do not
hesitate to go back to easier lessons. Above all
things, do not worry your puppy by doing too
much at a time.

The great secret of making your puppy steady
at his drop is never in these early lessons to call
or whistle him up to you from his drop; always
go back to him and give him a reward or a pat
on the head before you release him.

### DROPPING TO FUR.

If you are fortunate enough to have an
enclosure containing a few rabbits or Belgian
hares, or even have a tame rabbit that you can
let out of its hutch on to a grass field, you can carry
these lessons of early puppyhood still further.

Your lessons in dropping to command and hand
have not been so much an object in themselves
as the stepping stones to general steadiness in

the field, of which the principal element is dropping to fur.

Assuming that you have such an enclosure as is indicated above, or have let out your tame rabbit, go and fetch your puppy and put on him a light but strong cord, two or three yards long —you will previously have accustomed him to some such restraint. Lead the puppy quietly up to within a yard or two of the rabbit—which will probably be feeding in the open—and make him stand there. If he shows any inclination to have a go at it, check him gently but firmly with the cord.

As soon as the rabbit moves—if it is very tame you will probably have to poke it up with a stick or your foot—drop the puppy with your usual " Up," and in case of need press down his hindquarters with your hand ; go away from the puppy so far as the length of the cord, which you will still hold in your hand, will allow, and if he attempts to get up before you give him the command, drop him again in the exact spot that he has left.

In course of time you can leave the puppy dropped, walk from him without the necessity of still holding the cord, and work the rabbit gradually nearer to him, always taking care that he is not allowed to get up until you come right back to him and give him the command.

The only object of these lessons is to teach

the puppy to drop to fur—to convert his natural inclination to chase into some other movement—and to remain dropped in the face of temptation.

As soon as these objects are attained, these lessons should be given very sparingly, and only often enough to prevent the puppy from losing the habit he has contracted and giving play to his natural inclination.

Tame rabbits and Belgian hares rarely make seats, and to persevere too far with lessons on them is to encourage your puppy to hunt with his eyes and not—as he should of course do—with his nose.

If, however, your enclosure contains also wild rabbits, you can carry these early lessons still further; in fact, you can make him hunt in the enclosure just as if he were hunting in the field. Whenever he finds one of the tame variety he will stand it as usual and drop as it goes away. Leave him dropped a minute or two, give him the command "Gone away," and start him hunting in a direction opposite to that which the tame rabbit has taken. He will soon come to understand that when a rabbit has been started and the command given he has no more concern with that rabbit, and will go on hunting without paying any attention to the rabbit he has started or other rabbits that he may *see* in the enclosure.

However steady your puppy may be in this enclosure, do not fall into the error of thinking that he is a broken dog. When you hunt him outside you will probably find that sooner or later he relapses into chasing on sight. You have, however, taught him by this enclosure work what he ought to have done, and will have little difficulty in getting him to understand that what he has been accustomed to do in the enclosure he must also do in the field. Moreover, you have not yet given him any but the most rudimentary lessons in working his ground.

### Waiting for Orders before Retrieving.

In the retrieving lessons advocated in the earlier part of this chapter nothing has been said about making your puppy wait until he has been told to go out to retrieve.

As soon as he goes out readily, picks up smartly, and returns to you at the gallop, you must begin this part of his education.

In some books on retriever breaking you are advised at this stage to put a check-cord on your puppy, hold or put your foot firmly on the loose end of it, throw the bundle or other object as usual, and when, as usual, the puppy goes out to retrieve, let him be pulled up—probably "turned turtle"—as soon as he gets to the limit of the check-cord. This has always seemed to me a somewhat barbarous and illogical proceeding, and one calculated to damp most effectually the puppy's eagerness to retrieve. However this may be, it is not, in my opinion, the way to treat a very young puppy. Better postpone this part of the puppy's education until he will drop and stay where you have put him fairly consistently, in the meantime not doing too much of the going-out-to-retrieve-without-orders business ; you do not want this to become too deep-seated a habit.

The puppy, then, being fairly good at dropping and staying, drop him by your side, go out a yard or two in front of him, keeping your eye on him all the time, and, if he does not show any inclination to leave his drop, throw the object in a direction away from the puppy, raising the other hand and if he attempts to move giving him your usual " Up," come back to your puppy, give him a reward or pat on the head, and send him out with your usual " Fetch it."

If, despite your precautions, the puppy does get up before you get back to him, block his way, catch him, take him back, drop him again where he started from, and leave him dropped there while you go and pick the object up yourself; if you can prevent it without frightening him you should not let him retrieve the object under these circumstances ; although—so far as you have taught him at present—he has not committed any fault in going to retrieve without orders, he has committed one in leaving his drop and it is this fault that you should not condone.

If, however, circumstances are too strong for you and the puppy slips past you, do not run after him, but treat the matter as if the puppy had done all right ; but next time be more careful to prevent his going out until told—throwing the object from the puppy's side while you gently hold him down with your other hand.

From time to time throw the object and go and pick it up yourself, leaving the puppy at the drop, and not letting him get up until you give him leave.

As soon as you can rely upon your puppy not going out to retrieve without orders, gradually increase the distance you go from him before you throw the object, and alter the direction from time to time. The spot on which the object is thrown should always be one where the puppy will have to use his nose to find it ; subject to this, it is a good plan at first to throw the object in such a way as to enable your puppy to see its general direction—so you will be laying the foundation for " marking " the fall. These lessons can be varied by going out of sight of the puppy before you throw the object— you can begin to teach him to work to your hand—or starting a trail (*see* p. 62), sometimes in and sometimes out of his sight.

In all these lessons never send your puppy to retrieve until you have come right back to him and given him the command; if he leaves his drop without orders, never fail to put him back in the exact spot and to go away from him at least as far as you went originally before coming back and letting him go.

# CHAPTER IV.

## OTHER METHODS OF TEACHING RETRIEVING.

So long as your spaniel is not too old to learn, the initial retrieving lessons indicated in the last chapter are applicable to puppies or dogs of any age. If, however, they are postponed much longer than early puppyhood days, your dog will have developed a will and ideas of his own.

If your dog will pick up the object you have thrown for him, but despite all your adroitness will not come back to you with it, you must have recourse to the check-cord. Let this be light, but strong—you will find that super woven line answers this description and also does not knot—and between 5yds. and 10yds. long.

Let him trail the check-cord for a few days to get accustomed to it, sometimes leading him by it. Throw the object as you would have done to your puppy, and, when he gets fairly hold of it, gently play the dog up to you with the check-cord, walking or running slowly away as recommended in the last chapter and giving a reward. Gradually make less and less use of the cord, but keep it on for some time so that, in case your dog shows his old disinclination to come up to you, you still have the cord to fall back upon.

The method employed in these lessons so far has been to start by throwing something for the dog to fetch and to induce him to bring it back to you either with or without a check-cord.

There is, however, another quite distinct method which starts from the other end of the business. It consists of first getting the dog to walk by your side carrying the object in his mouth and not throwing the object for the dog to retrieve until he is perfect in this. This method is insisted on by Sir Henry Smith in his excellent work on " Retrievers and How to Break Them," and is one that I have used with success. You must first get your dog to walk to heel on a very light and short cord—a piece of salmon line meets the case—and to stop at command (*see* Chapter X.). In the fullness of time dangle the object you have selected for this lesson before the dog, until he takes it from your hand—if he will pick it up from the ground let him do so. If you find one object distasteful to the dog you must try another and another until you perchance hit upon the right one—just as is recommended in the last chapter in the case of a young puppy which refuses to pick up the knotted pocket-handkerchief. If you have a broken dog that will readily take and carry the object, have him out and give it him to carry—for the example and encouragement of the novice.

As soon as your novice takes the object from your hand, continue to walk on with him for a few yards and stop him, put your hand down very quietly—any sudden movement will probably make the dog drop the object—and stroke his back. Repeat this walking, stopping, and stroking two or three times before you take the object, and when you do take it be careful to take it in the manner recommended in the last chapter, *i.e.*, by putting your hand underneath his jaws and pressing the object upwards and towards rather than away from his mouth, at the same time telling him to " Give it."

It is, perhaps, hardly necessary to say that the reason why you do not take the object from the dog every time you stop him is that you do not want him to regard it as a matter of course that whenever he stops he is to give the object up; if you keep him in uncertainty as to whether on any particular stop he is to give the object up or not he is less likely to fall into the objectionable habit of dropping it on the ground. If he does drop the object from time to time and seems disinclined to pick it up, pick it up yourself, let him take it from your hand, and, without moving from the spot, take it straight from his mouth.

Dogs under training by this method are generally those which are not by nature keen on lifting or carrying anything, and on this account are apt to drop their stuff ; be therefore sparing with any *edible* reward and use it only so far as is necessary to impress upon the dog's mind that, when he holds the object until you take it from his mouth, he has done well, and when he drops it, ill. In time you will, of course, dispense with any cord and make the dog walk to heel, carrying the object, and will stop him occasionally and sometimes take the object and sometimes not, but do not make him carry the object far without taking it from him ; if he gets tired of it, he will drop it—just the thing you want to avoid.

As soon as you find that he will carry the object by your side and hold it until you take it from him, throw the object for him to fetch and continue his retrieving lessons in the manner suggested in the last chapter, taking particular care to let the dog come up from behind you to the position of "heel" ; you should also keep him waiting before you take the object from him ; and now and then make him walk at heel with it and stop a time or two before you let him give it up.

If the dog refuses to take any object from your hand, your only course will be to open his mouth as gently as possible, put the object into

it, and hold it there, and repeat this whenever
he drops it.

If even this fails you had better get rid of the
dog—if retrieving is a *sine quâ non.*

Although there is still another method of
teaching retrieving, generally called the French
method, this is only likely to be successful in the
hands of an accomplished breaker—for whom
these notes are not intended ; in the hands of a
novice it is almost sure to entail unnecessary
hardship on the dog and result in failure at
the end.

Assuming that by the employment of one or
other of the methods suggested in this chapter
you have overcome your dog's disinclination to
pick up the object and bring it back to you, his
subsequent education can be carried out on the
lines indicated in the last chapter. He must be
taught to drop to command and hand and stay
where dropped until told to go, to use his nose,
to wait for orders before going out to retrieve,
and, if there are the necessary facilities, to drop
to fur. All the suggestions for teaching these
and other matters mentioned in the last chapter
can be adopted in the same way as if you
had successfully taken your dog in hand in
early puppyhood. Unless, however, your dog
is an exceptionally shy one, you can relax, to a
slight extent, your scrupulous attention to the
rule against any display of harshness.

# CHAPTER V.

## DROPPING TO SHOT; ANSWERING TO WHISTLE; "BACK."

### DROPPING TO SHOT.

HAVING, by the graduated series of lessons suggested in Chapter III., taught your dog to drop to hand, it is a very short step to getting him to drop to shot.

Buy a cheap Belgian revolver and a box or two of blank cartridges ; load your revolver, upraise the pistol hand and snap off a cartridge as you do so. If the dog is looking towards you when you raise your hand, he will probably be down at the moment you fire ; if he is looking the other way, he will turn towards the noise, and seeing the upraised hand will, as usual, drop to the well-known signal.

In time he connects the shot with dropping and goes down whenever he hears it and whether you raise your hand or not.

Although spaniels are not often troubled—at any rate permanently—with gun-shyness, it is best to be on the safe side.

Prior to beginning the above lessons, get your dog accustomed to the noise of the report by snapping off your pistol at some distance from his run or getting an attendant to do so ; if the dog shows any signs of nervousness, put off the dropping to shot lessons until, by having it snapped off at a gradually decreasing distance from the dog, or as a signal for meal-times, and by making much of him by way of encouragement, you have dispelled all trace of nervousness.

### ANSWERING TO WHISTLE AND "BACK."

When you come to shooting over your puppy, you do not want to spend the day with an artificial whistle between your lips.

Although it is useful to have such a whistle in your pocket or hung on your coat—as a last resource—you will have to rely in the main on the sound produced by your own unaided mouth, and it is this sound—or rather combination of sounds—that is here referred to. Nothing disturbs game so much as the human voice, and you must therefore teach your puppy to answer to your whistle

The occasions on which you will want to whistle to your dog may be divided roughly into (a) when you want to attract his attention, e.g., to turn him when he is hunting; and (b) when you want him to come back to you ; and it is most useful to have two different notes or combination of sounds for these two different occasions, *e.g.*, a single low whistle for the one and a more compelling series of notes—something like that produced by a pea whistle—for the other.

Teaching your dog to come back to you when you whistle presents no difficulty. Drop your dog, walk on leaving him dropped and seeing that he does not move even an inch, and, having gone some little distance, whistle him up, and, when he comes up to you, give him a reward.

Up to now you have never let your dog leave his drop until you have gone back to him; if, remembering his former lessons, he does not come to your whistle, call him by name and encourage him to come up to you.

You must be careful not to overdo these coming to whistle lessons; if you do, he will gradually lose his steadiness at drop. For every time that you whistle him up from his drop, make him stay dropped until you return to him at least twice as often. When he has once learned the meaning of your whistle—which he should very soon do—do not drop him before whistling him up, but seize occasions when he is some way from you and reward him whenever he comes up readily.

In connection with these lessons it is useful to teach your dog the meaning of the word " Back " in preparation for his lessons in

hunting.  When you are out with your dog
on a road, and have let him go on in front of
you, stand still and give him the command
" Back," supplement this with his name, and give
him a reward when he gets back to you.  If
desired, the use of this word may be subsequently
dropped, and the dog taught to come back and
hunt nearer to you by a less compelling variation
of your " Come in " whistle.

As to your low whistle to attract your dog's
attention, any definite lessons are generally
unnecessary ; the dog soon understands what
you mean when it comes to hunting.  If thought
necessary, you can give your low whistle—
supplemented by his name—when the dog is
near you and offer him a reward, or can throw
your reward on the ground away from your
dog, give your whistle, and work the dog up to it.

# PART III.—SUBSEQUENT BREAKING.

Up to this point it is possible for all the lessons to have been given in a paddock, and most of them on a lawn, and there is no reason why a puppy of six months old should not have been made perfect in them, although his owner has not access to an acre of shooting.

The supreme importance of this preliminary education is shown when you look back at what you have achieved. You have taught your dog nearly all the necessary words of command ; he will drop to hand and shot, and also, possibly, fur, and will remain at his drop until told to go ; he will retrieve a dummy rabbit at a gallop right up to hand, and will wait for orders before doing so.

Although for the sake of clearness, and in order to meet the case of those who have not continuous and easy access to ground where some rabbits or game may be found, this division into Handbreaking (Part II.) and Subsequent Breaking (Part III.) appeared advisible, it is not, of course, essential. The two parts really merge into one another and form one gradual system of education.

With those who have spaniel ground at their doors, the puppy should grow up with his work, and in his earliest days would, at odd moments, be given a chance of getting scent into his nose, would be encouraged to face cover, and be gaining some idea of hunting to his master; in other words, most of the suggestions as to hunting contained in Part III. would have been carried out before the Handbreaking is completed. If this course, however, is adopted I think it important that any chance of the puppy chasing should be avoided; on the one hand you do not want to quarrel with the puppy in these early days, while on the other hand a chase left unrebuked is sowing the seeds of trouble in the future.

# CHAPTER VI.

## RETRIEVING.

FROM this point in his education onwards the
dividing line between handbreaking and work
in the field gradually disappears. It is well,
therefore, either before or during your lessons
on hunting, to carry his retrieving lessons from
the dummy rabbit up to the real article. This
is a step that I, personally, always take with a
certain amount of trepidation, and endeavour
to make the change as little abrupt as possible.
Your dummy rabbit has been cold and stiff, so,
therefore, should your first real rabbits be. In
addition to this, you can mitigate the shock
your dog will receive on coming up to the
unaccustomed object by putting your dummy
rabbit in a fixed spot for a time or two, and
putting your first cold rabbits in that same
spot.

Take care, also, that your first rabbits are
small ones, and are free from any external
blood, and are so placed that the back of the
rabbit will first present itself to the dog as he
comes up to it ; you want him to carry it well in
his mouth, and not by the skin. With the sole

exception of the change of object, change
nothing else ; whistle him up to you if he has
grown accustomed to this ; stand still or retreat,
as the case may be, and take the rabbit from him
in exactly the same way as you have acted in
the case of the dummy.

Continue the lessons with cold rabbits until
he brings them as well as he did the dummy,
change to one that you have just killed and
placed for him to bring, go on to one that he has
seen you shoot when at heel, and finish up by
one that he has found ; at first, however, let
each rabbit you send him for be dead and have
ceased to kick.

The system suggested above of placing any
object new to the dog in a spot from which he is
accustomed to retrieve can be applied to every
species of feather he will be called upon to
retrieve in the field, and is especially useful to
counteract the dislike so many dogs have to
lifting woodcock and snipe.

I suggest carrying on the above lessons with
rabbits for several reasons. If you use your
spaniel as a general purpose dog these will be
his chief fare. At field trials he will be principally
tested on them. Partridges will probably not
be available at the time of year you want to
introduce him to his real business, and even if
available are not generally so easily come at as
rabbits ; if you prefer them, and circumstances

permit, by all means start on partridges and
come to rabbits later on.

On the subject of laying trails, breakers of
retrievers and spaniels are not in entire agree-
ment. Some breakers eschew them altogether,
and consider their own foot-scent an efficient
substitute ; some never lay them with the
retrieving bundle, but wait until such time as
the puppy has had his first lessons in retrieving
the real article and lay them with that ; some
lay them with a rabbit skin, others with the
retrieving bundle slightly scented with aniseed,
others, again, with the retrieving bundle pure and
simple.

In deciding for yourself this question of laying
trails you must remember that you have to
break your spaniel off most foot-scents when he
is hunting, and consequently must have some
means of teaching him—on receiving the appropriate command—to pick up and follow the foot-
scent of wounded fur or feather. Whether you
use a dead partridge or rabbit, a skin or a
bundle, it is long odds that if you drag it by
your side, your dog will take your own line
rather than the one you have laid for him—
when laying trails, from time to time carry the
object instead of dragging it, and watch the
result.

Although this ability to take your own foot-
scent at a gallop may have some value, it leaves

much to be desired. Various devices have, therefore, been adopted with the object of avoiding confusion of your own scent with that of the object dragged. It may suffice, for a time at least, to get someone else to drag the object in the ordinary manner, and let him get well away before you bring up your dog; you may by juggling with a long line, a series of posts or trees, and a wide detour on your own part, succeed in laying a trail some distance away from your own; or, a more simple matter, you can attach the object to the end of a fishing rod by a short piece of string, and if you desire to make assurance doubly sure, get someone else to lay the trail with this.

If it appeals to you, you can teach your dog to go back for anything that you have dropped, whether he has seen you drop it or not, and, incidentally, thus teach him to stick to the line of your own foot-scent. Drop the object—at first in his sight, afterwards unknown to him—and take him on an ever-increasing distance before you send him back for it. It is said to cultivate the memory, it is certain that it is useful to hurry up a dog that is getting slow in his return—he does not like being left behind.

It is not my intention to dwell at length upon your spaniel's introduction to the various phases of the retrieving business in the field. There are many excellent books on retrievers, and

what is sauce for one is sauce for the other.    A
few hints may, however, be useful.

Do not send a young dog to retrieve feather
unless you are sure that it is down and, at first,
also dead, nor a rabbit unless you are sure that it
is either killed or so disabled as to be unable to
reach its burrow.    You want to impress upon
your dog that the stuff is there to find, if only he
looks long enough.

Do not send him for everything you kill.

Do not shoot a rabbit he has found unless he
drops.

Do not shoot too close.

If your dog is at fault and looks back to you
for guidance, treat him as a man and a brother,
and do your best to help him—from where you
stand.

Finally, do not reiterate " Hie lost," " Hie lost."
If you have broken him properly, he should
know the meaning of the word as well as you.
Repetition of it is useless, makes him look a
fool, and, if he pays any attention to it, distracts
his mind from the business he has in hand.

# CHAPTER VII.

## HUNTING.

### ɪ.—IN COVER.

A SPANIEL that will not hunt gorse bramble and other punishing cover is not worthy of the name. These are just the very places where his utility is most conspicuous and in which a good dog is well nigh indispensable. It is also a part of a spaniel's work in which puppies—even of the same litter—differ to a surprising extent.

Apart from those puppies who seem to have inherited the knowledge, you will have to teach your puppy that it is in such sanctuaries that game is to be found. It is not probable that a spaniel loves thorny places or desires prickles any more than you or I. It is only when he has learnt that they hold what his soul desires—the scent of fur or feather—that his enthusiasm rises superior to our own. The way to teach him to work the thick is not to push or pitch him into it, but to show him that it is game-holding cover and leave the rest to him.

A spaniel that is accustomed to work and find only on open ground is not likely to quest among what he has grown to believe are unprofitable thorns. You must first teach him that they often hold the stuff, and you can best do so by the usual appeal to his appetite, and by beginning as before with easy work.

Take your puppy to some standing bracken or other high prickleless cover; throw in a bit of biscuit—let him see you do so at first—and tell him to " Get in " ; gradually extend his investigations to more forbidding-looking cover, usually selecting that through which there is a rabbit run. In his investigations after biscuit he will from time to time find rabbits, and, after having once learnt that rabbits are to be found therein, should never thereafter be shy of prickly cover. In teaching these lessons an old dog which is keen on rough stuff is a very useful adjunct. Send him in where rabbits are likely to be found and your puppy will soon follow.

## 2.—IN THE OPEN.

In Chapter II. we have seen that when working in the open a spaniel should hunt all the ground within fifteen or twenty yards on each side of the gun, first hunting all likely cover on one side, then crossing in front of the handler— still hunting—and working on the other side, then back again, until he finds or the beat is finished ; that this should be done up or down wind, at the best pace of which the dog is capable without overrunning his nose, without unduly dwelling on foot-scents, without missing any ground, and without a word or whistle from his handler.

How to bring about this result is the problem you have to face. Up to the present you have not given any handbreaking lessons directed to this object, and in consequence you will find that the inculcation of a proper method of hunting takes more time than preventing your dog chasing or retrieving without orders. It is also the part of your dog's education in which you will have to rely to a greater extent upon your own judgment as applied to the particular dog you are breaking. The following notes must, therefore, be taken as the merest suggestions.

The first question that presents itself is as to whether you are to give the first lessons on ground where there is no scent and nothing to find or on ground where there is a certain amount of stuff.

Places where there is likely to be much stuff can be ruled out at once. You do not want to be under the necessity of continually dropping your dog and so checking him in his work, nor do you want your dog to think that he must be continually finding stuff and so lapse into the habit of "chucking it" if he does not find soon.

The practice of spaniel breakers varies, I believe, materially on this question of ground; some start quartering lessons on bare grass, force their puppies to make short beats, and rely upon pace, style, keenness, and use of nose coming later.

Some use a check-cord and some do not.

Personally I prefer ground where there is something for the dog to find, endeavour to do without the check-cord, and rely mostly upon showing him that the handler is helping him to attain his object and pleasure in life, *i.e.*, the finding of stuff, and consequently is not acting merely as an arbitrary taskmaster.

The chief difficulties you will encounter at the start are, first, preventing the dog going straight out in front of you instead of quartering his ground; secondly, preventing his going out too far on each side of you or, in the case of some puppies, getting him to go out far enough; and, thirdly, preventing him dwelling on unprofitable foot-scent. It is in order to meet these difficulties that it has been suggested in previous chapters that you should teach your dog the meaning of " Back," of your low whistle, and of " Gone away."

In the earlier lessons be sparing of any command likely to check the dog, unless a very bold one, and do not insist upon too exact a compliance with your wishes in the matter of method of working his ground. These lessons must, like the handbreaking lessons, be made easy at first, be very gradually worked up to the point of instant and absolute obedience, and culminate in your dog's ability to work his ground entirely on his own.

The ground-work of your lessons on a proper method of working—for want of a better word herein called quartering—is the inclination of your dog to follow you wherever you go, and his natural instinct, if he has it, to quarter the wind.

Start your beat, therefore, straight into the wind and quarter it yourself in short beats; by holding your hand out, preferably not very far from the ground, and other encouragements, get your dog out beyond you in the direction across the wind that you are going; as soon as he has got out, give your low whistle and turn sharply in the contrary direction across the wind, and hold your hand out in the new direction; as soon as your dog has come across you and gone out beyond you, turn again sharply across the wind, give your whistle, get your dog across and beyond you and repeat these movements until the end of the beat. This sounds rather complicated, but the general idea may be gathered from the following diagram, in which the thick lines approximately represent your own track and the dotted lines those of your dog, your

beat beginning from the bottom of the diagram.
If you can so arrange your beat that somewhere
about each of the points A, A, A, A, A, &c.,
there is a small gorse bush or small patch of

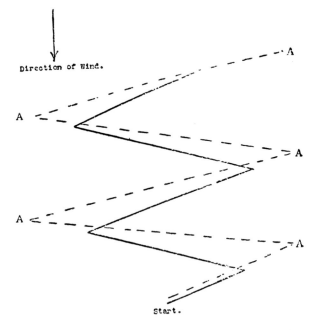

Direction of Wind.

Start.

rushes, bracken, or other likely cover, you will
make your task the easier.   In your lessons on
hunting thick stuff you will have taught your
dog that these are the places where rabbits are
to be found, and if, in addition to holding your

hand towards them, you give your well-known "Get in," it is more than likely that your dog will race across you towards the first of them, and, having worked it, will turn to your whistle the more readily when he sees that you are directing him to another similar patch.

If your dog will not turn to your low whistle, you will have to call him by name, or resort to your more compelling human or artificial whistle ; each time that he begins to turn to this, repeat your low whistle. It is this low whistle that you want your dog to connect with turning.

You may also find it useful to *start* your dog hunting with your low whistle as well as holding out your hand, and also from time to time to take him within 10yds. or so of a rough patch that he knows and start him into it with this low whistle and pointing hand combined. This should help him to connect your low whistle with game-holding cover, and to understand that when he hears it he must turn to you for directions as to where this cover is.

The diagram set out is only intended to explain the general nature of your first lessons in quartering. It is not intended that it should be followed in detail. The angles of your own quartering may be more or possibly less acute, you may find that you can get your dog to go well out from you across the wind without making your own quarterings so long, and I sincerely hope that your dog will not—at any rate after the first lesson or two—quarter with the regularity shown by the dotted lines; if he does, and the ground holds any scent, he has probably got no nose.

The greater tendency your dog displays to work on in front of you instead of quartering his ground, the more acute you should make the angle of your own quarterings—in other words the more nearly you should come back on the line of your last previous beat. This, and the fact that you are working up wind—which at first should be your invariable rule—should go far to meet the first of your difficulties.

This tendency to work on straight ahead should also be further counteracted by the use of your " Back." Up to now your dog has learned that this command means that he is to come straight back to you. If, whenever you use it when he is hunting, you hold your hand to one side with an inclination somewhat behind you, he will soon learn that it means that he is not necessarily to come straight back to you but is only to hunt nearer to you on the side your hand indicates.

As your dog gradually gets to understand what is required of him, make your own quarterings shorter and shorter until at last you are walking in a straight line up your beat with your

dog quartering his ground and working a strip—
with yourself in the middle—at least thirty yards
wide.

Always, too, keep him going at a gallop, even
if you have to run yourself. Although a spaniel
should know where his handler is and work
accordingly, he should go at the gallop all the
time and only see his handler out of the corner
of his eye. Whenever he stops to see where
you are, whistle him across you; keep him
bustling all the time.

So far your third difficulty, *i.e.*, preventing
your dog dwelling on unprofitable scent—
generally foot-scent—and so getting into the
habit of "pottering," has not been dealt with.
If, as I suggest you should do, you are giving
your hunting lessons on ground where there is a
probability of your dog finding something, there
is sure to be a certain amount of scent—even if
it is only a rabbit run—and your dog, we hope,
is equally sure to acknowledge this scent. On
the one hand you do not want him to take up
a line that leads to a burrow perhaps a quarter of
a mile away; on the other hand you do want
to encourage by every possible means his
thirst for any scent that may lead to a rabbit
in its seat or even up to a rabbit that is crawling
on a yard or two in front of his nose.

This being so, your action when your dog
acknowledges a scent during these early lessons

must depend partly upon the natural qualities of the particular dog you are breaking and partly upon whether you consider the scent likely to be profitable or not. If the dog is dwelling upon what is obviously a rabbit run or a place which clearly cannot hold any stuff, call him off immediately with your " Gone away," and hunt him away from it. If there is any doubt about the matter, call the dog off immediately if he is inclined to potter; if, however, he is naturally a fast and keen worker, you can give him more time to investigate the scent, and so decide the matter for himself. The safest rule is, I think, to err rather on the side of calling off your dog too soon than on that of letting him dwell upon the scent too long—pottering in a gundog is an abomination to be avoided at all hazards.

If you experience much difficulty in getting your dog to turn to your low whistle, it is not a bad plan to take him on to ground where there is no scent, start him off—still up wind—to one side of you, and only let him go out a few yards on each beat before insisting on his turning to your whistle, gradually letting him out farther as he improves in this respect. A dog will often turn to command at five yards away, although he refuses to do so at fifteen ; but in this, as in all other lessons, the rule should be that the nearer the dog is to you, the more subdued should be your whistle or your voice.

If you habitually shout at a dog that is near you, you will need a megaphone to enforce your commands when he is far away.

*Check-cord.*—If despite all your expedients your dog still refuses to turn to your low whistle fairly consistently, you will have to hunt him on a check-cord between ten and twenty yards long as a last resource, and turn him by this means, using your low whistle as an accompaniment to the pull of the cord. The best material, as stated in an earlier chapter, is a thin variety of what is known in the trade as " super woven line." Although this is strong and light and, being woven instead of twisted, does not kink, it will, nevertheless, be a continuing vexation to you. If you hold the end, your dog will wrap it round a clump of rushes or get it caught up in some other obstruction ; if you let it go free, the end will never be anywhere near you when you want to catch hold of it to turn your dog, It will get caught up—sometimes you will step on it yourself—and bring your dog to a full stop just as he is beginning to go nicely, and, by creating chaotic confusion of his ideas, make him go in a hesitating and uncertain manner, and check all pace and dash. With this picture of horror before you and its dire accompaniment of loss of temper on your own part, postpone its use until every other expedient has failed ; if you have once been driven to it, no words of mine will, I am sure, be needed to induce you to dispense with it as soon as possible.

*Dropping.*—As soon as your dog goes out readily and quarters fairly, make a point of dropping him and leaving him dropped a minute or two before you start him hunting, and give him the signal to hunt with, say, a click of your tongue and a hand directing him as to whether he is to go out to right or left. If you are breaking two puppies, and are likely in the future to work them as a brace, it is useful to accustom one to start out always on the right and the other on the left.

As your dog improves in his quartering, drop him by command, and subsequently by shot, from time to time, sometimes when near you, sometimes when well out, sometimes when on the outward and sometimes when on the inward tack, and see that he drops without hesitation, and does not move until you start him off again with your low whistle or " Gone away." It cannot be too often pointed out that this dropping instantaneously wherever he may be is the foundation of steadiness. If he will not do so when there is no strong counter attraction, you will never get him to do so when a rabbit is legging it in front of him.

*Chasing.*—This brings us to the question of what you are to do when in the course of his lessons on hunting he starts a rabbit.

If his handbreaking has been finished off by teaching him to drop to fur, as suggested in Part II., there is no reason why he should not of his own accord drop to the first rabbit he finds —most of my own puppies do so. There will, however, possibly come a time when he throws all his handbreaking lessons to the wind.

This will probably occur when he has got on to the scent of a rabbit that is crawling along in some such cover as rushes in front of him. Both dog and rabbit are on the move, and in the same direction; the dog is gradually overtaking the rabbit; eventually the rabbit takes to its heels in earnest, and your dog's feelings get the better of him.

Whenever your dog fails to drop a rabbit on his own account, you must do your best to drop him to command; if, despite your attempts, a chase occurs, stand still, wait till the dog comes back—if he has been well broken up to this point he will have his tail between his legs in acknowledgment of his fault—take hold of him, drag him to the exact spot where he should have dropped, and having dropped him there go some distance away from him—I generally sit down and light a pipe—leave him dropped for a minute or two at least, or longer if he seems unrepentant, and do not let him leave his drop until you have gone back to him. In the case of an obstinate but nervous dog, the " taking hold of him " may be the rub. If this difficulty occurs, in future hunt him with a check-cord only just long enough to enable you to get him up to you—a yard or two should suffice—and keep this on until you find that you can dispense with it.

*Down Wind.*—So far nothing has been said about hunting down wind. The reason for advising that all the first lessons in quartering should be given up wind is that, when working down wind, a spaniel's inclination to go out straight in front of you instead of quartering his ground, and to get out too far at that, is much more pronounced. It may be that his desire to get away from your scent has a lot to do with it.

Do not, therefore, ask him to hunt down wind, except at rare intervals and not for long at a time, until he quarters his ground fairly well up wind. When you do begin the down wind lessons, be particularly careful to start him off to one side as usual, and try to get him well out and so counteract his tendency to turn sooner than usual and to go straight down wind instead of crossing you. If this tendency asserts itself, stand still, give your usual " Back," and work him by your hand towards and across you; do not walk on until he has got level with you; at the same time do not let him work behind you into the wind, unless he is obviously on a scent.

The most effective method of working a spaniel down wind is a matter of opinion. Personally, I do not object to him going well out down wind and working his ground up wind back to me. If he works down wind in the same way as up, I am generally suspicious of his nose.

It is, moreover, unreasonable to expect the same pace in a spaniel working down wind as you would when he is quartering up wind; in the one case he has to search for a scent, in the other it is coming on the wind straight to his nose.

Similarly, you should not expect your spaniel to go at the same pace at all times and on all ground   One day and place may be good scenting, and another bad; a good dog knows this and regulates his pace accordingly.

If your dog goes well up wind and down, a cross wind does not present much difficulty.   In a diagonal head wind he will, however, naturally quarter the wind, and it is well to prevent his quartering taking him too much behind you, and consequently to whistle him across when on such a tack sooner than you would if the direction of the beat were straight into the wind.

*Within Gunshot.*—In all quartering lessons, especially up wind, aim at whistling your dog across as soon as ever he has reached the limit you have decided on as the distance he is to go out from you, and stick to this limit.

A spaniel has to spring his game within gun-shot of you, and the length of his quarterings has consequently to be determined with reference to you and not the nearest hedge or wall. This turning to whistle is only a prelude to the dog turning at the proper distance on his own initiative. If you whistle him across sometimes at five yards and others at fifty he will never get a confirmed range, and you will have to whistle him across to the end of the chapter.

Your eye will soon tell you when your dog has got out as far as you like him to go; if, whenever he gets to about this distance, you whistle him across you, he will in time learn to turn of his own accord at the same distance. Do not, however, rely too soon upon his having acquired a confirmed range, and even after you think he has acquired one, whistle him across from time to time; very few dogs are so good as not to require a whistle to turn them on occasions, and the obedience to your low whistle that your dog has learnt in his early days may easily be lost by disuse.

*Missing Ground.*—When your dog has once learnt to quarter his ground fairly well, take special care that he does not miss any ground that is likely to hold stuff. If you see that he has not brought, say, a small gorse bush within the range of his nose, do not go up to it and kick up any rabbit it may hold; insist upon

your dog coming back to investigate it himself.
When out "Spanieling"—sometimes even at
field trials — there is nothing more annoying
than to see your dog baulked of a find by some
officious foot.

*Standing Rabbits.*—If you want your dog
to stand his rabbits, and he does not do so
naturally, or in consequence of your final hand
breaking lessons, you may be able to effect your
object by stopping him (*see* Chapter X.) as soon
as you see that he is drawing up to the seat.
If this fails, find a tenanted seat yourself, bring
your dog up to it upwind on a check-cord, and
with a continuous strain on the check-cord prevent
him from dashing in, and make him stand.

Whether your dog stands his rabbits of his
own accord or has to be taught to do so, do not
at first let him put them out himself. Whenever you can, make him stand for thirty seconds
or so, and put the rabbit up with your foot. Be
careful to make him drop as soon as ever the
rabbit starts ; with this object in view, place
yourself in such a position that you can press
him down with your hand in case he should fail
to drop of his own accord or to command.
Many spaniels stand rabbits naturally, but if
they once give up this habit it is a difficult job
to get them to do so artificially. I once spoilt
a promising puppy by letting him put them up
himself at too early a stage in his education.

G

At first he stood naturally, but through my mismanagement took to dashing in and trying to catch them—a fault which I was never able to eradicate.

### 3.—IN HEDGEROW.

The reader will, no doubt, have gathered from the above remarks, if his own experience had not already taught him, that the proper working of open ground is not easily attained. The difficulty of attaining it is only equalled by the ease with which it may be lost.

Do not, therefore, risk its loss in the early days by allowing your dog to indulge in his inclination to go out in front of you, which he must of necessity do when working a hedge. Useful as this accomplishment may be on many rough shoots, postpone it until he has acquired a confirmed range, and, at any rate during his first season, use him for it sparingly.

The inborn love of hedge-hunting that most dogs have may be useful to you in testing your spaniel's obedience in turning to whistle; you may work him on a beat bounded on one side by a hedge, and let him work a few yards of it before you whistle him across, and insist that he obeys.

When the time is ripe for hedge work, you should find your "Get in" enough to induce your dog to work it from your own side.

You may, however, desire to teach him to work from the far side. In such case select a hedge over or through which you can see him, get him across with " Over "—throwing a piece of biscuit will soon teach him the word—stop him when he has got far enough ahead of you, and make him wait until you get almost abreast of him and have given him leave to go on. In a short time an intelligent dog will put his head through every gap or thin place in the thickest hedge to find out where you are, and will wait until you come up with him. If the dog comes through to your side of the hedge without orders, make him get back the same way he came.

As you are on one side of the hedge and your dog is on the other, you are, of course powerless to prevent him going right ahead, unless you have previously taught him to stop on command. You can, if you like, drop him in your usual way ; as, however, your inability to enforce his dropping if he disobeys is likely to weaken his obedience to that command, it is better to use a distinct command, such as the hiss suggested in Chapter X. Every time he disobeys this, call him in, and make him stop under circumstances where no prickly hedge prevents you from enforcing your commands.

# CHAPTER VIII.

## WORK WITH THE GUN.

THE foregoing notes cover, I think, all single work except the carrying and use of the gun. In the earliest lessons on quartering it is no use hampering yourself with anything more bulky than your Belgian revolver and a few blank cartridges. You will want this to continue the lessons on dropping to shot, but until your dog quarters boldly, be sparing of its use. If before this period arrives he gets slack about dropping to shot, continue his lessons in this at times when you are not hunting him rather than run the risk of cramping his style.

The period at which you begin to carry a gun when hunting will depend largely upon the dog. You will soon discover whether he goes better with a gun or without and will act accordingly. Whichever way it may be, your ultimate aim is to get him to go equally well in either case. Do not, therefore, always carry a gun, on the other hand do not always be without one. At field trials for spaniels the handler is not allowed to shoot, but is allowed to carry a gun if he so

desires.    It is, however, an awful nuisance
lugging a gun about all day as well as your dog.
It is well, therefore, to get your dog to work to
you and not to your gun ; if he is not accustomed
to this you will find that at field trials he will
work to the gun carried by the official shooters,
who are appointed to shoot the stuff, and not to
you, and on that account will be more difficult to
handle and be apt to miss much of the ground
on your allotted beat.

Having a gun in your hand, use it to drop your
dog in lieu of your pistol ; that is to say, drop
him to it from time to time when there is
nothing to shoot at.   By no means shoot anything unless your dog has dropped to it or has
not seen it.    It is one thing for your dog to be
steady to a rabbit going away unharmed, and
quite another thing for him to remain at his drop
when he sees it suddenly bowled over and—in
legal phrase—" reduced into possession."    For
this reason, do not shoot a rabbit to him when
hunting until you have many times let off your
gun wide of rabbits that he has started, and he
has been cured of any inclination to run in to the
combined effect of the rabbit and the shot

When you do begin to shoot to him, do not let
him retrieve the first rabbit—possibly the first
twenty rabbits—that you kill.   Leave him
dropped, go and pick up the rabbit yourself,
come back to him with it and do not let him stir

until you are ready for him to go on with his beat.

The principle that you are seeking to instil is that, when you kill, your dog is not necessarily to retrieve. If you send him every time, he begins to connect the kill—and ultimately the shot—with retrieving, and disregards the intermediate step, *i.e.*, your permission to go out.

The temptation with every novice at breaking is to "practise" his dog in retrieving every time he kills or thinks he has. If there is a sure way of throwing away the fruits of all the earlier lessons, it is to give way to this temptation. Just as the maxims "Breaking is only a figure of speech" and "The preliminary course is by far the most important" are essential to the making of a good spaniel, so are these other maxims, "Do not send your dog for everything you kill" and "Do not shoot unless your dog is down," essential if you would not mar him when made. The first of these should be observed during the whole of your spaniel's sporting career. Strict observance of the second may be confined to his earlier years.

So long as your spaniel shows the slightest inclination to retrieve without orders, look to see whether he has dropped before you get your gun up, and do not shoot if he is not down; even if he is down, let the rabbit get well away before you let off your gun. A miss may result, but a few extra rabbits in the bag are no compensation for the spoiling of your dog.

You must not, of course, send your dog to retrieve immediately you have killed a rabbit. Leave him dropped until he has thoroughly settled down; the more eager he is to go, the longer you must keep him down. Observe this rule still more rigidly if the rabbit is only legged. The temptation to make sure of adding one more to the bag may be great, but you must resist it. If you yourself have not self-control, you cannot expect your dog to acquire it.

If your dog shows any inclination to go in without orders, do not let him go until you have come up to him, and patted his head, in addition to giving him your usual command.

If, despite due observance of the above maxims, you should find great difficulty in getting your dog steady to shot, do not let him hunt; keep him at heel—as a last resource trailing a check-cord—see that he drops to your shot, and send him to retrieve but seldom. Also take him ferreting; drop him by your side, if necessary pegging him down with a check-cord just not long enough to enable him to reach the burrows; when the check-cord has spun him once or twice, he ought to cure himself.

If your dog, though steady, is getting sloppy in his retrieving, only hunt him often enough to keep his hunting right. Use him as a retriever

whenever opportunity offers.   Many keen game-
finders come to regard the retrieving business
as rather a bore, and are impatient to get on
hunting again.

At the beginning of a season do not expect
your dog to be as good as he was at the end of
the season before.   Put him through a modified
course of handbreaking before the season opens ;
you will save much loss of time and temper, and
the possible ruination of your dog.   When it
comes to his first day in the field, shoot over him
carefully—assume that he intends to chase every
rabbit, run every foot-scent, and go in at every
shot.

# CHAPTER IX.

## BRACE AND TEAM WORK.

WHAT is needed in a non-retrieving brace or team is summed up in the Field Trial Regulations of the International Gundog League Sporting Spaniel Society as follows :—

" They are expected to beat their ground harmoniously together."

In the case of a retrieving brace or team it is also requisite that one of them, or in some cases such one of them as the judge may name, should be sent by the handler to retrieve, and that the rest should not leave their drop—they will have dropped to shot—until the retrieving dog has done his part, and the order to go on hunting has been given by the handler.

No breaker is likely to essay to handle a brace, still less a team, until he has become an experienced handler of a single spaniel, and as these notes are not intended for the experienced handler, short ones on the subject should suffice.

So far as I have been able to discover, no printed suggestions as to brace and team work soar beyond the expedient of one or more whippers-in—in some cases mounted—to control an unruly pack. This method is so opposed to all the principles of breaking advocated in previous chapters that it is of itself sufficient excuse for including the subject.

The lessons leading up to steadiness at the drop while another dog is retrieving in reality form part of handbreaking, and, in consequence, the second of the two above-mentioned requisites for good brace or team work will be taken first.

As soon as—but not before—any two of your spaniels will individually remain at their drop until you go back to them or call them up to you, these lessons can begin.

Take these two dogs—A and B—out to their usual schoolroom, drop them both, call A up to you by name—not whistle—reward him when he comes up with an edible gift or pat on the head, and drop him; go back to B and, if he has remained down, reward him also, leaving him dropped.

If, when you call A, B also comes, take B back to the exact spot on which you dropped him, and, remaining near enough to him to put him down with your hand if he attempts to move, call A again. If B has not moved, then reward him; if he has moved, repeat the process, and do not reward him until he stays where you dropped him. Reverse the process by calling B and leaving A dropped. If you have an old dog that you can rely upon to remain dropped until you go back to him or call him up, it will be the easier to teach the novice what is expected of him. You want him to understand that whether he comes to your call —which he will be eager to do—or remains where you dropped him—which he will not like —he eventually gets the reward. For this reason, you can from time to time omit any edible reward in the case of the dog you call, and give it only to the one you leave dropped.

As A and B become perfect at this business, take out one or the other of them with another of your proposed team, and repeat the performance. As soon as your team is perfect in this in twos in any combination, introduce a third dog, and so on until you can have the whole of your team perfect in staying dropped while one of them is called up to you. At the end of the later lessons allow all your dogs to leave their drop simultaneously with your " Gone away " or some other signal appropriate to continuing to hunt.

Having reached this stage, take your retrieving bundle, drop all your dogs—if they are all in a bunch, get them nicely scattered by calling them up and dropping them individually—throw your bundle here and there among them, but do not let them touch it. If they seem steady at this, go away some distance and throw your bundle, come back to your team, none of which ought to have moved an inch, and call one by name. The first time or two he will probably come up to you instead of going to fetch the bundle, but a whispered " Fetch it," so that the rest of them cannot hear, should soon show him what you want. When he has done his part, go up to each of the other dogs and reward him at his drop. Repeat the proceedings with the other dogs in your team.

In all these lessons it is best to send out the dogs that are steadiest at their drop before those that are less steady ; but be careful not to get into the habit of sending them in any fixed order, or you will find your team inclined to adopt this order on their own account, instead of waiting for their names.

Be careful also always to send a dog by name, and to avoid, even when working the retrieving dog, the use of any action or command such as " Fetch it," or " Hic lost," which you have taught your dogs to obey individually but have not taught them to disregard unless coupled with their names. Above all things never pass over the least slackness at remaining at the drop until released.

The foregoing lessons, although specially directed to brace or team work, may be usefully employed with all your spaniels, even if you

only intend to work them single.    They inculcate
general steadiness and self-control, go a certain
distance towards lessening jealousy, and are
especially useful during the off season, or such
other time as your dogs are short of work in
the field.

If your team is intended to be a non-retrieving
one, you will, of course, omit the above lessons.
Whether a retrieving team or not, you will
have to instil in them the second requisite, *i.e.*,
beating their ground harmoniously together—
including never getting out of gunshot, being
steady, and missing no ground.    Whether you
wish for a retrieving or non-retrieving team
will depend upon yourself.

A team composed of dogs that are never
asked to retrieve have not as strong a temptation
to run in to shot, and are thus easier to steady.
Moreover, in a non-retrieving team you possibly
will not want any of its members to drop to
shot or to fur or feather ; in that case freedom
from chase is all that will be required in this
connection.    On the other hand, no member of
a team so broken is fit to run single as a general
purpose dog, and if you are likely to want to
use your team spaniels in this capacity, you
will be obliged to keep a greater number of
dogs than would otherwise be the case.    This
consideration, coupled with the fact that on
such occasions as you want to take out a

retriever you need not ask your retrieving team
to do anything but hunt, should turn the scale in
favour of a retrieving team.

There are two methods of working a brace—
this applies in a modified degree to a team. You
can either have one dog working all the ground
on one side of you, *i.e.*, turning when he comes
up to you instead of crossing you—the other
working similarly on the other side; or you can
have both dogs quartering the whole width of
your beat and crossing both you and each other.

If either of the dogs in your brace will be
wanted for single work, the latter is the best
method ; it is only continuing when in company
with another dog the same method of working
his ground that you have taught him when working single. The former method has also the
disadvantage that, if you indulge in much
brace work, each dog when working single is
inclined to work on one side of you only instead
of boldly quartering across your front.

Whichever method you employ, do not ask
any of your dogs to form one of a brace or team
until you have perfected him at single work.
When you have achieved this, your only
difficulty will be to counteract any faults he may
contract through jealousy, such as rushing up to
another dog that is feathering on a scent, getting
too far ahead in order to work his own ground,
or going to retrieve when another dog has been

called.   The first you will be able to counteract
by calling off the peccant dog by name and
working him away, the second by your usual
" Back " preceded by his name, the last by an
application of the lessons suggested in the
earlier part of this Chapter.

Any repeated misbehaviour by a member of a
brace or team caused by jealousy must be strin-
gently dealt with.   The fault *ex hypothesi* does
not arise from ignorance, and amounts to a
defying of your authority, which you cannot
afford to pass over.

Do not expect your spaniel to go the same
pace in a brace or team as when working single
—two or more dogs are beating much the same
ground as one dog has been accustomed to
cover.   You will probably find that when first
given such work they will need a certain amount
of steadying down.   This fact, and the fact that
you will have to avoid bunching by calling your
dogs by name—if you whistle, they will all come
—should make you chary of giving a dog in his
first season much brace or team work.   When
working him single you want him to go at his
best pace and to turn to your low whistle ; every
time you use his name to turn him, this latter
habit weakens.

# CHAPTER X.

## ODDS AND ENDS.

1. WATER.—It is not because the subject of water work is a negligible quantity that no mention of it has been made before or that it is at last included in a chapter of such a miscellaneous character. The real reason is twofold —in the first place, it runs through the whole of both the early and later lessons, and so a definite niche for it is hard to find; in the second place, my lines have not been cast in a country which lent itself to the higher branches of water work, and as all that has gone before has been garnered out of my own experience I hesitate to embark on a dissertation on the subject. A few suggestions, however, may be useful.

In the introduction Mr. Arkwright writes that most Spaniel puppies take to water naturally, but not all of them. There is nothing more certain than that if they do not take to it naturally you will never give them a love of it by pushing or throwing them in. Cajolery, not force, is the means you must employ. Choose a warm day—the hotter the better—and take your puppies to the gently sloping edge of a stream or pond, get their interest aroused in a piece of biscuit and throw it into the water so that they can seize it without going out of their depth; if one of them is bold enough to enter the water and grab the biscuit, throw in other pieces and emulation may encourage the shyer ones; if none of them enter, steer the biscuit nearer to the shore or throw in another piece so that it is within reach if they wet their toes. Gradually increase the distance and aim at leading each puppy to swim by dropping each piece in front of him and further towards deep water than the last. Do not expect to accomplish this all in one day, and each time you take them to the water start the lesson with a biscuit they can easily reach. If each time you also take with you a dog that knows the business, so much the better.

There are several alternatives to the above. If your water is a stream across which you can wade, ford it yourself and encourage the puppy to follow you; if a pond, the puppy may follow your boat.

As to your subsequent procedure, much depends upon what facilities for lessons in water you may have. If you have an island on to which you can throw a biscuit, your course is clear; if some reeds which hold water hens, your spaniel's keenness on hunting them out should make him disregard any fear of water he may have. Whatever method you employ in early days, the ultimate aim is to get him into or across water on command, and the biscuit method lends itself admirably to this. Drop him on the bank, throw in your biscuit, and only allow him to go in and get it on command—invariably the same.

From the nature of the ground on which most Field Trials for spaniels are held, water tests are often impossible, and for this reason breakers who live in a district where water work is not required on their own shootings are apt to pay little attention to this branch of breaking. A spaniel has more duties to perform than a retriever, and such a pitch of perfection in the higher branches of retrieving out of and across water can hardly be expected of a spaniel as is required of a retriever. Even if this is so, competitors at Field Trials may be sure that whenever possible their spaniels will be tested as to their readiness to enter, to hunt across and to retrieve from water, and so far as the International Gundog League (Sporting Spaniel Society) is concerned, all doubts as to this have been removed by a recent alteration in the Field Trial Regulations.

2. IT may be useful to recapitulate the words

of command you have been recommended to teach your dog. They are :—

Fetch it (*see* p. 32).
Gently (*see* p. 35).
Hie lost (*see* p. 37).
Up (*see* p. 39).

Gone away (*see* p. 41).
Back (*see* p. 56, 72).
Get in (*see* p. 66).
Over (*see* p. 83).

3. In addition to these you may add "Sit," to drop your dog by your side; "Lie down," to make him lie at length in a grouse butt, &c.; "Wait," to prevent him going through a gate or over a fence before you. The teaching of these should present no difficulty, if you adopt the simple expedient of using gentle force to make the action follow the word.

4. It will be useful, also, especially in teaching hedge work, if you make your dog stop—not necessarily drop—to a hiss. You can teach the dog to obey this when by your side by the above simple expedient, and if he does not of himself do it when away from you, by the aid of the check-cord. With some dogs, I have found a hiss so like the sibilant in "Sit," that they have naturally dropped to it. If you like, you can easily substitute a hiss for your "Up." It disturbs less game, but, on the other hand, is less compelling, and seems to be inaudible in a high wind.

5. "HEEL."—I have purposely omitted all mention of this in the earlier chapters. Some

H 2

dog-breaking books advise that a lesson on walking to heel should be one of the first you give your puppy. Personally, I think this is a great mistake, and if limited to a choice between the two would make it the last rather than the first. The whole of your breaking has been directed to encouraging and controlling dash and pace, not checking it. There is, however, no doubt that a spaniel's education is incomplete until he has been taught it. He should be so broken as to be capable of being used as a retriever pure and simple. Put a short check-cord on the dog, and give your lessons on the road. Start with the check-cord in your hand and the dog by your side; whenever he leaves your heel, give him the command and enforce obedience by a jerk on the cord. When he is beginning to understand, drop the cord from time to time, and let him trail it; whenever he begins to forge ahead, step on the cord, and bring him up with a jerk, at the same time saying "Heel." If you eschew a check-cord, you can teach him "Heel" in any narrow lane or path, by using a walking stick or cutting whip to prevent his getting ahead. Use it only to control his movements, not, of course, to chastise him. Carrying an attractive dainty in your left hand, and from time to time rewarding him, is a valuable adjunct to—possibly a substitute for—either cord or stick. If, through inadvertence, you have let him get in front of you, do not run after him; stand still, make him come to heel and stay there a moment or two before you walk on.

6. KENNEL DISCIPLINE. — The correct performance under temptation of what you have taught your dog depends so much upon his self-control that you should leave no stone unturned to fortify it. When your dogs are coming from paddock to yard, or from yard to kennel, do not let them all push through in a disorderly throng as soon as the gate is opened; make each one wait until his name is called. So at feeding time, let them come to their bowls or trough only in answer to their names. It matters not whether they are kennelled singly, or in twos or more; make him or them get on the bench, put the food down with a " No," and let each dog come to it with a " Yes " prefaced with his name. Even the pet-dog trick of " Trust " and " Paid for " is not to be despised if you substitute for these words a " No " and " Yes." A clear understanding of the meaning of " no " is of the greatest use in the field, especially if, in retrieving, your dog is to your knowledge taking up a wrong line.

7. JUMPING.—Teach your puppy to jump as soon as his legs are fit for it. You do not want to have to lift him over any obstruction you

come across when shooting, and which you can get over easily yourself. He will jump naturally to a certain extent, but it is surprising to what a degree his powers in this respect can be improved. A home-made frame with sliding transverse panels fitted across some convenient gate or door way is all that you will want. Start with the lowest panel in and the others out, and from time to time add further panels to increase the height. In connection with these lessons teach him the meaning of " Over."

Finally, insist upon your spaniel effacing himself in a railway carriage, car, or trap, and not annoying other occupants. If you have him in the house, prepare a place for him in some secluded corner of each room, and see that he retires to it and stays there until allowed to leave it.

# PART IV.

## CHAPTER XI.

### PSYCHOLOGY AND DOG-BREAKING.

In breaking a spaniel—and the same remark
applies to a retriever or any other dog, whether
a gundog or not—it must be remembered that
although the aim of dog-breaking is the control
of the dog's bodily actions, this can only be
effected through the medium of the dog's mind.
It is, therefore, the mind and not the body of the
dog with which we are primarily concerned;
any direct contact with its body—such as
chastisement, "spinning" it with the check-cord
as the finale of a chase—is only of value so far
as it affects the dog's mind. It is equally true
that if any such direct bodily contact is to have
the desired effect of "stamping out ' any action
we desire to inhibit (*i.e.*, absolutely repress), it
is essential that the punishment and the crime
be clearly connected together in the *dog's* mind;
that they are so connected in *our* minds only is
without value. Few breakers are aware that the

dog's mind, in common with that of other animals, has been scientifically studied and that many patient observations and careful experiments are recorded in an extensive literature on the subject of "Animal Psychology." It is remarkable that the accepted principles of dog-breaking—which in most cases have been arrived at empirically and handed down by tradition—are to a great extent in accord with the scientist. This chapter is a first attempt to nterest breakers in the subject.

In nearly all pursuits the tendency of the day is to seek for principles and reasons, and an enquiry into them may be of interest in itself; the application of the principles may be of practical value as forming a clue to the occasional non-success of the old empirical methods and as suggesting to the breaker original and possibly more successful methods of his own; finally, the breaker of gundogs, dealing as he does with the dog mind on the plane of its natural tendencies and its predominant interests, is in a far better position to observe certain phases in the development of the animal mind than the scientist whose observations are usually made on animals under the condition of experiment and so of unnatural restraint.

Although the scientist abhors mere anecdote, he is at the same time conscious of the great disadvantages accompanying test conditions, and recognises the value of observations and suggestions of the breaker when founded on a careful record of fact. Thus Professor Lloyd Morgan states : " Under domestication we seek to bring about a new working adjustment to conditions imposed by man. The skilful trainer utilises instinctive tendencies as a basis, and by a system of rewards and punishments leads the *intelligent* modification of behaviour along the lines directed by his deliberate purpose. The conditions are largely those of experiment, and they bring out the play and range of *intelligence* in a way that would otherwise elude our observation." The italics in the above quotation are my own and are specially to be noted.

So far as their observations on animals under test conditions go, the majority of psychologists draw a sharp distinction between the lower or *intelligent* stage of mental development and the higher or *rational* stage. They define intelligence as the power to learn by experience, they use the word reason as pointing to something more than this, namely the power to found upon experience and appreciate and apply a general scheme. Intelligence may enable a dog or a horse, by an extended series of trials and errors, to learn to open a particular gate or door, but it would require the exercise of reason to enable it to appreciate the fact that the latch of a door is the crucial point, and so be in a position to open all gates or doors provided with any ordinary latch. The same distinction may be applied to the processes of the human mind : " If to prevent a boy sucking his thumb we administer bitter aloes, we trust to *intelligent* control through the immediate effect of experience, but if he be induced to give up the habit because it is babyish he so far exercises *rational* control " (Lloyd Morgan). Psychologists generally allow to animals the possession of intelligence, but deny or do not admit the possession of reason ; they hesitate however to assert that in no animal are there the beginnings of a rational scheme, and it is on this that dog-breakers with their exceptional advantages might be able to throw some light. For the breaker's observations to be of any value it is, however, necessary for him to accept the terminology current among psychologists.

The meaning of the expressions used in this chapter having, I hope, been made reasonably clear, the next step is to enquire as to the mental material on which the breaker has to work. This would appear to consist of INSTINCT, INTELLIGENCE, and the FEELINGS and EMOTIONS of the dog. As to Reason, it seems safer to follow the psychologists and not to assume its existence.

INSTINCT is an inherited tendency in the

nature of a blind indiscriminating impulse, and its first exercise must necessarily be prior to the individual's experience.   Its characteristics appear to be :

(*a*) It may be, and in almost all cases is, modified by experience.

(*b*) It may not manifest itself until the animal has reached a certain age, in such a case it is called " deferred."

(*c*) Its development may be retarded by disuse.

(*d*) If it does not meet with satisfaction, it may, in the individual, gradually wane and disappear.

(*e*) The less deeply-ingrained it is the more easily can it be modified, the sooner it lapses, and the more practice it requires to become established as a habit.

Very little consideration will be needed to see what a wealth of suggestion the above afford to the breaker.   Take for instance " chasing," the bugbear of many breakers, and the downfall of many a good dog.   Personally, I have never come across a young puppy that would chase the first rabbit it saw.   In my experience, therefore, the impulse to chase is a " deferred " impulse.   Is it not then possible to prevent it ever manifesting itself in chasing ?

Throughout the early chapters of this book I have preached the doctrine of breaking young, and this, to my mind, may afford an answer to the question, though it appears to go a step further than the psychologists would go   The final hand-breaking lesson advocated to induce steadiness is in the rabbit-pen (*see* page 42). Is it too far-fetched to suggest that the dropping whenever a rabbit moves displaces the inchoate impulse to chase, that such impulse though still unmanifested is modified by the puppy's experience in the pen, that finally the reward of the biscuit and the approbation of the breaker make dropping a more satisfactory response to the movement of the rabbit than a chase.

There are other instances of " deferred " instincts.   I always test my young puppies as to their retrieving capacity before they are ten weeks old and at the first attempt have invariably found that they will gallop out for a knotted handkerchief (thrown only a very short distance), immediately pick it up and gallop straight back with it.   The earliest age at which this has been accomplished is five weeks and one day.   At that age, the puppy, however keen he might ultimately become, showed no inclination to hunt and would not even acknowledge the line of a rabbit that had just moved away.   It would seem, therefore, that the hunting instinct is a " deferred " instinct, although the carrying instinct is not, and this reversal of what would seem the natural order of things—one would have thought that an animal must catch a thing before he could carry it—was very puzzling until it was pointed out that a vixen would bring a rabbit to the earth, break it up, and leave the cubs to carry off their portions.

How suggestive, too, is the characteristic that the development of an instinct may be retarded by disuse. I once had through my hands a spaniel that had spent the first 12 or 14 months of its life in preparation for the show-bench. When first I had it out it took no interest whatever in a scent or showed the smallest inclination to hunt, though I must confess it retrieved a bundle very nicely. By letting it run wild in standing bracken in company with a keen wild dog, it gradually "came to," and by no means disgraced itself in the field the following season. I cannot help thinking that if the opportunity of exercising its hunting instinct had been longer delayed, this instinct would have completely lapsed. The question of what effect this lapsing in the individual would have upon the offspring is a difficult one and outside the scope of this chapter.

Note also the last of the characteristics above set out. May not this afford some answer to the question why some dogs are more difficult to break than others? The chasing instinct may be deeply ingrained, and so be the more difficult to cast out ; the hunting or carrying instinct may be slight, and so the more practice be required to attain perfection; the tendency to a hard mouth (if it can be classed as instinctive) may not be deeply ingrained, and so be the more easily modified.

INTELLIGENCE: *i.e.*, learning by experience.— A distinction has been drawn above (page 105) between "intelligence" and "reason" as these terms are understood by the majority of psychologists. Intelligence has also apparently to be distinguished from a lower form of experience-learning, *i.e.*, "automatism," exemplified in white rats learning to find their way unerringly through a model of the Hampton Court maze. This form of experience-learning does not seem to carry the animal beyond the actual labyrinth in which it learnt and, as gundogs work on various grounds and under divers conditions, may, I think, be disregarded even in the case of a spaniel acquiring a confirmed range.

In what way then does intelligence (*i.e.* experience-learning) work? It works in exactly the way that common sense would lead us to expect, *i.e.*, all those actions that are accompanied or closely followed by pleasure or satisfaction (including success) are stamped in, whereas actions accompanied or closely followed by discomfort (including non-success) are stamped out.

In the classical experiments (Thorndike) a

box was constructed with a door which fell open
on (say) pulling a string, a plate of fish was
placed outside the box and a cat imprisoned
within ; in its impulsive struggles to escape, the
cat happened to claw the string, and thus *by
chance* opened the door, sallied forth and ate the
fish. The cat was again and again similarly
imprisoned, the useless struggles gradually
became fewer and fewer until at last the cat, as
soon as it was put in the box, straightway pulled
the string and walked out. All the useless
actions had been stamped out and the one
successful action stamped in. In other words,
the experienced cat as soon as it was put in the
box " responded " to the situation by pulling the
string, this action alone being associated in its
mind with release and food—the accomplishment
of its desires.

In our breaking a similar process goes on, but
as we have, or ought to have, an organised
scheme—ourselves selecting the situation (*e.g.*, a
rabbit moving off) and selecting the response we
desire (*e.g.*, dropping)—and have at our command
the means of inflicting either satisfaction or
discomfort at will, the matter is to that extent
simplified.

Whether, however, the animal entirely teaches
itself or is taught by us, the following matters
are material :

(*a*) The association in the dog's mind of satisfaction with the response we desire to encourage, and discomfort with the response we desire to inhibit.

(*b*) The amount of satisfaction or discomfort.

(*c*) The closeness in point of time and the preciseness of the connection between the response and the satisfaction or discomfort.

(*d*) The frequency with which the response we desire is connected with the given situation and the duration of each such connection.

(*e*) The readiness of the response to be connected with the situation.

(*f*) The fact that to your dog a " situation " is at first a complex matter consisting of many elements in addition to the one element to which you are teaching him to give the desired response.

(*g*) It is easier to obtain the response you desire *de novo*, than to get rid of a response already established and form a new one.

I fear that the above sound terrifyingly obscure, but trust that the comments and instances immediately following may afford some measure of illumination.

The first question that naturally arises is as to the comparative advantages of stamping in the desired response by satisfaction (such as a reward), or stamping out all other responses by discomfort (such as punishment). A consideration of (*c*) above, will afford a partial answer to the question.  Your spaniel runs in to a very strong running cock-pheasant, hunts it up and returns triumphantly to you with the pheasant in its mouth.  In lieu of the approval it expects, the dog is met with chastisement or hard words; the last thing it has done is to retrieve to hand, and it is undoubtedly the retrieving to hand, and not the running in to shot, that your chastisement, if often repeated, would stamp out, leaving the running in possibly unaffected.  So, too, the chastisement of a dog that comes back to your whistle after a prolonged chase is neither sufficiently closely or precisely connected with the running in to steady him, whereas, if he had been made to drop and been rewarded, both the conditions of closeness and precision would have been fulfilled.  Moreover, rewarding for good behaviour rather than chastising for bad is far more likely to preserve the good relations between you and your dog, on which the success of your breaking so much depends.  As to the above, scientists consider stamping out the more effective, but the divergence of opinion is explained by the fact that the discomfort they inflict upon the subjects of their experiments usually takes the form of an electric shock, the administration of which actually accompanies the response to be inhibited.  Moreover, the preservation of good relations between them and their subjects is, of course, immaterial.  My

I

advocacy of stamping in the desired response is, of course, not intended to be universal. It applies, in my opinion, to the education of young puppies. In the case of older dogs that have already contracted bad habits, such as chasing or running in to shot, the breaker will perforce be thrown back upon stamping out; in these cases, "spinning" the culprit in full career with the check-cord, hauling him back and dropping him, should effect a cure; it satisfies the conditions of closeness and preciseness which subsequent chastisement can never do; it also precludes the possibility of that most awkward of breaking conundrums—your action if your dog runs in and retrieves to hand.

The nature and optimum amount of satisfaction or discomfort (*b*, on page 112) has also received some attention at the scientist's hands (Thorndike). Senseless and severe chastisement engenders fear; by fear a dog may be broken but never educated, and such a course of conduct results in a cowed and useless dog, however steady he may be to the actual breaker. In addition to spinning with the check-cord, taking the culprit home and bringing out another dog, leaving him tied to a fence, or any other punishment that deprives him of the pleasure a keen dog takes in accompanying his master and the gun, will, in many cases, bring the crime home to him. As to satisfiers, an edible reward, if kennelled alone his master's company, his master's approval by word or deed, should be enough, and the better the breaker the better are the terms on which he is with his dog, and consequently the more force will the approval have.

As our breaking is analogous to the formation of a habit, no comment is needed upon the necessity of frequently connecting (*d*, on page 112) the response (say dropping) with the given situation (say a rabbit moving off).  On this point scientists, moreover, tell us that a slightly satisfying response made often may win a closer connection than a more satisfying response made only rarely (Thorndike).  This being so as to stamping in any desired response, it would appear to be equally true as to stamping out responses we desire to inhibit, and corresponds with the practice of most breakers who prefer to have a dog out for a short time every day rather than have him out for seven times as long on one day and then leave him for a week.

The duration of the connection, too, needs little comment.  We all know that if a dog drops to shot and is *immediately* sent in to retrieve, he will soon give up dropping and run in.

The readiness of the response to be connected with the situation (*e*, on page 112) is most strongly emphasised in the case of forming a connection between going out to retrieve and "fetch it"

or some similar command. It is also at the root
of the statement (*see* page 71) that a dog turns
more readily to your whistle if he sees that you
are working him across to game-holding cover.

The consideration referred to in (*f*), on page
112, is of great importance to the breaker,
although it does not appear to have received
from scientists the attention it seems to me to
deserve. It cannot be too strongly emphasised
that the breaker must at all hazards have everything connected with his breaking clear cut and
well defined in the mind of his dog. Animal
consciousness has been described as a "big
blooming buzzing confusion," and it rests with
the breaker to reduce this to orderliness by
segregating and clarifying the situations and
responses he desires.

It is a common experience that a spaniel may
be perfectly steady when handled by its breaker,
but wild with a strange purchaser, and, if the
purchaser is a bad handler, continue wild to the
end of the chapter. There are also, I believe,
instances in which the only Belgian hare in a
pen a dog chased was a fresh one introduced in
place of one that had died. It is, moreover,
common knowledge among breakers that a
spaniel may consistently drop to a moving rabbit
in a pen and yet chase the first one that moves
off outside it. The explanation of the last
phenomenon—and a similar reasoning applies

to the other two—appears to be this.  In the mind of the breaker the situation in the pen to which the spaniel responds by dropping is the rabbit and that alone ; in the dog's mind, however, the situation is a compound one, consisting not only of the particular rabbit, but also of the breaker, the pen itself, the bushes it contains, the wire enclosing it, and maybe a hundred other elements.  It is only by keeping constant a rabbit and the breaker and varying the other elements of the situation that these two alone come to form a situation, or the elements of a situation, to which the dog gives the desired response.

The above considerations undoubtedly lie at the root of the advisability of having more than one pen—a fact which breakers have discovered empirically—and also underlie the dictum that it matters little that a dog should chase when the breaker is not present.  Everyone who has tried to break a confirmed chaser will heartily subscribe to (*g*) on page 112.

ATTENTION.—Although each of the matters (*a*) to (*g*) (page 112) have been dealt with seriatim, there is one other important matter to be considered which so far has been pre-supposed.  In Chapter I. occurs the sentence "Never give a lesson unless you have your puppy's whole attention, or continue one when you have lost it."  This injunction is, perhaps, the most important of the whole series. It is absolutely essential that the puppy should have his attention concentrated on you, your commands, and the response you wish him to connect with such commands. If his attention is elsewhere your lessons are next to useless. Most, if not all, of the best breakers attach so much importance to this that they never dream of giving the early lessons when a third party is present, or in a spot where counter-attractions are likely to present themselves.

The practice of breakers is in accordance with the conclusions of scientists, some of whom assert that the difficulty they have experienced in teaching a cat to open the door, referred to on page 111, by themselves holding the cat's paw and putting it through the performance is due to the fact that the cat's attention was not directed to the necessary act but rather to freeing its paw from their grasp. Lack of attention may, as suggested above, arise from extraneous circumstances; it may also be caused by the puppy's state of mind. Its capacity for giving the necessary attention may be impaired by fear of the breaker, by ill-health, by boredom, or by exhaustion; the first of these emphasises yet again the importance of preserving good relations between yourself and your pupil; most highly-strung dogs, moreover, need quiet hand-ling; if you shout to enforce your commands their tails go down and they seem to lose their heads and become incapable of responding to your signals and commands. As to the last of the above, I find that a spaniel that is not absolutely steady is—contrary to what one would expect—more likely to run in when it is tired than when first put down.

So important a factor in their experiments do scientists regard this matter of attention that it has been suggested that animals destined to participate in certain experiments should be subjected in their youth to a course of training in the habit of giving attention (Smith). As applied to our breaking this suggestion is of even greater importance, and I cannot help thinking that the hand-breaking lessons suggested in Part II. are of value not only in teaching the specific matters there set out, but also affording some such general course of training in attention as has been suggested above.

INTEREST.—Closely allied to Attention is the question of Interest. The matter is considered of no little importance by scientists, many of whom argue that it affords an explanation of what at first blush would appear to be cases of reflective imitation. In breaking, too, it should not be overlooked, and might perhaps have been considered in connection with the previous remarks on a complex situation (pages 112 and 116).

It is evident that the dam is a centre of

interest to unweaned puppies, food to them when
weaned, scent of game to the gundog; in the
case of social animals like the dog, the members
of the herd are centres of interest to each other.
I think, too, there can be no doubt that the good
breaker becomes a strong centre of interest to
the dog he is breaking—possibly the more
readily if he feeds the dog himself.

In a natural state, no doubt the interest which
in puppyhood was centred in the dam shifted,
as the puppy grew older, to his companions in
the pack. If you start handling a puppy as soon
as it is weaned you introduce yourself as an
interest before interest becomes centred in the
rest of the litter, and if you subsequently kennel
the pupil by himself you obviate a division of
interest and attract the more of it to yourself.
This solitary kennelling is widely advocated,
and the reason given is that the dog is thus in
a better position to think over and digest the
lessons it receives; this is, however, I think,
presupposing a mental equipment higher than
that to which the dog can possibly lay claim.

In the presence of more than one centre of
interest behaviour is different to that which is
manifested in the presence of only one.

If a worm is thrown to a chicken when alone
it proceeds to deal with it forthwith; if a worm
is thrown to a chicken in the presence of companions the lucky one seizes it, and, instead of

devouring, runs off with it. In the case of exceptionally keen dogs which during hand-breaking have been eager for a biscuit as a reward for dropping, I find that when they drop to a rabbit in the open the rabbit proves so strong a centre of interest that they ignore the biscuit.

If the average Field Trial winner were allowed to go off and hunt on its own, I think there is little doubt that instead of dropping it would chase every rabbit it found; that it is steady when the breaker is present as an additional centre of interest may well be due to some such cause as that indicated above.

Some shooting men seem incapable of break-ing for steadiness, or even preventing a broken dog from becoming unsteady, and this may in part be due to their failure to become a centre of interest to the dog, and thus modify the pre-dominant interest represented by the rabbit. What factors go to make the breaker the centre of interest to the dog I am unable to suggest; if, however, the training is not an absorbing interest to the breaker, it seems improbable that he will be a centre of interest to his dog; if also he does not watch his dog his dog will not watch him. Possibly, too, this interaction of centres of interest may account for some dogs being specially difficult to break; in their case the rabbit may be so overmastering a centre of interest as at first to leave no room for the breaker being of any interest whatever.

FEELINGS AND EMOTIONS.—Breakers are almost unanimous in insisting that breaking must be adapted to the particular character and disposition of each dog ; one dog is shy, another bold ; one is highly strung, another stolid ; one responsive, another self-centred ; one docile, another wilful ; each must be treated with such and similar characteristics in view. These are all matters for the personal observation of the individual breaker, and as to them no help can be expected from scientists, though even some of them criticise the earlier experiments on the ground that sufficient attention did not appear to have been paid to the "animal equation."

---

The works referred to in this chapter are :

" Mind in Animals," by E. M Smith (Cambridge University Press), which contains a full Bibliography.

"Animal Behaviour," by C. Lloyd Morgan (Edward Arnold).

"Animal Intelligence," by E. L. Thorndike (Macmillan & Co.).

# CHAPTER XII.

## FIELD TRIALS.

IF you have a spaniel of exceptional natural ability, and have perfected him in his work in the field; if also you have succeeded in attaining such perfection without in any way impairing his keenness, dash, and pace—having laid to heart and applied the principles and methods of breaking herein advocated, you have, I warrant, so attained it—your dog is a certain Field Trial winner, and I hope that you will give him the chance of proving himself such.

You will perhaps have heard or read suggestions that Field Trial work is not practical work, that it is something outside the sphere of sport, that it is in the nature of a trick performance, that there is some mystery about the making of a Field Trial dog, that one breaker can and another is unable to put on the "polish" necessary to get even a certificate of merit. Do not believe a word of it; these are the vapourings of the ignorant or the embittered.

It is no doubt disappointing to take to Trials what you consider to be a perfect spaniel, and find that your pet is "outed" on the first round.

Assuming that your dog's work comes up to
your expectations—which is not usually the case
—your failure is probably due to a misappre-
hension of what a perfect spaniel is, what
natural qualities are requisite, and, more par- ·
ticularly, how these natural qualities can be
preserved and encouraged, and yet the dog be
as steady as a rock. It is, I think, sometimes,
this perfect steadiness that blinds the eyes of
new comers to Field Trials to the game-
finding qualities. They know only two classes
of spaniels—the one a steady flat-catcher, the
other a good nosed game-finder but as wild as
the proverbial hawk. Steadiness combined with
game-finding and dash has never come within
their ken, and they are apt to jump to the conclusion that the combination is impossible.
The steadiness is obvious, therefore the game-
finding capacity must be absent is their illogical
conclusion.

I do not think that I should be far wrong in
saying that ninety-nine out of every hundred
spaniel owners who have never seen Field Trial
work have not the remotest conception of how
much can be got out of their dogs in the field,
or of how they should handle to make the most
of them; still less how these objects are to be
achieved.

Field Trial "polish" does not exist—in the
sense, at any rate, that it can be put upon a dog

broken on wrong lines. " Polish " is on the surface ; fitness for Field Trials, which is only perfection of work in the field, must go right through, and be built up from the start. To break for Trials is to break for sport. Success in breaking for sport spells success at Trials.

If you have never been to Field Trials, it is improbable that you know what your dog will be called upon to do. Go to them as a spectator, if possible, before you run a dog. You will never regret it. Even if you do not come to run a dog yourself, you will be amply compensated ; your eyes will be opened to further possibilities of your spaniel in the field, and, if observant, you may gain an inkling as to how to turn these possibilities into facts.

At the end of this chapter will be found a list of the societies holding Field Trials for spaniels at present in existence. Some of these Trials are open to all the world, others are confined to competitors residing or shooting within certain areas. The competition at these district meetings is necessarily the less severe, and the entrance fees are small. If possible, make your *début* as a competitor at one of these, but do not be content until you have flown at higher game.

The object of these societies is not only to develop the spaniel from a working point of view, to assist breeders in selecting the best working strains, and, by the granting of prizes and certificates of merit, to guarantee to purchasers that spaniels that have won them are in every way fit to shoot over and real good dogs at that. Their aim is also educational, and, although they are advertised as not being open to the public, anyone genuinely interested in the spaniel as a sporting dog should have no difficulty in obtaining from the secretary permission to attend.

First, then, attend as a spectator, if you can. If, however, you cannot, do not let this deter you from entering your dog.

If you piece together the sectional notes on the chapter on " The Perfect Spaniel " you will gain some idea of the work demanded of your dog. These are summed up in the International Gundog League Sporting Spaniel Society's Regulations as follows : " In all stakes the principal points to be considered by the judges are good nose, keenness, perseverance, obedience, freedom from chase, good style, courage in facing punishing cover, quartering the ground, so as to miss neither fur nor feather on the allotted beat. In single stakes, besides, the spaniels are expected to retrieve at command as required, tenderly, quickly, and right up to hand ; and any additional excellence, such as dropping to hand and shot, standing to their game and flushing it at command, &c., will be taken into account." As the spaniels are all

judged by " rule of gun," it is implied that all
noise on the handler's part is penalised.

Although the perfection of spaniel work is
that your dog should beat his ground without
any direction from you, a low whistle to turn
your dog or a whistle to hurry him up in his
retrieving is generally allowed. If you must
signal to him to turn him, accustom him always
to turn at this low whistle. Do not in the excite-
ment of the moment shout to him ; the judges will
conclude, and rightly, that a shout would have
been necessary to turn him in the field. It has
been pointed out in a previous chapter that even
when your dog will beat his ground himself you
should be careful to turn him to your low whistle
from time to time—lest he forget. When you
come to Field Trials you will thank your stars
that you have followed this advice. He may
have worked at home for days without a sound ;
Field Trial work—the disturbing influence of a
crowd, waiting his turn, perchance some excite-
ment caught from you—is quite another egg.

It is better to handle him to your whistle than
to let him miss much ground. Rabbits missed
and kicked up by the following crowd will put
him out as soon as anything ; they will be put
down to want of game-finding capacity and nose.
Next to this come pottering and lack of keenness, dash and pace. Persistent unsteadiness
and, of course, a hard mouth disqualify.

With respect to the Sporting Spaniel Society's regulations two remarks may usefully be made. The one is that at the recent meetings retrieving has been necessary in the brace and team as well as in the single stakes. Up to the present the requirement has been that one dog in each brace or team must retrieve. This tendency to introduce retrieving into brace and team work may be carried further—it has been so carried by some other societies. Before entering you should carefully read the conditions of the stakes; it may be that you will be required to send to retrieve such one or other of your dogs as the judges may direct.

The other remark is this. The entries at Spaniel Field Trials have grown to such a large extent, and the standard of work so much improved, that it has been found impossible to give an equal test in cover, hedgerow, and the open. As pointed out before, a spaniel is not worthy of the name unless he will face the thickest of thick stuff that you can find. This is still insisted on, and there are few judges that would not put the blackest of black marks against a spaniel that failed—personally I should like to see all competing spaniels taken to some such patch at the beginning of the meeting, tried in it one by one, and every one that failed to enter it readily disqualified forthwith. Although this disregard of punishment is essential, it is, from the nature of things, rarely that there is time for it to take the form of hedgerow work. Despite this, break your spaniels to it. It is often useful on a rough shoot, and at Trials you never know your luck.

Further rules of the same society enact : " In all stakes the spaniels shall be regularly shot over *in the customary sporting manner* and may be worked up and down wind, and on feather and on fur, and, where possible, in watᴇr, and no handler shall be allowed to carry in his hand either whip or stick "—a rule that in so many words disposes of the "circus" myth. The men who framed the rule were the men who originated Field Trials for spaniels and continue to compete and judge at them—gun-dog men, sportsmen all through, without an axe to grind. Would they have started and still support Field Trials unless convinced that they are in the interests of sport and for the practical improvement of the breed—among others—that they shoot over and love?

Although you may not carry either whip or stick, this prohibition does not prevent you carrying a gun. Take one with you if your dog hunts better to it, but leave your cartridges at home. All shooting is invariably done by guns appointed for the purpose.

The way the dogs are tried is laid down thus :—
" In single stakes, the judges will carry on the

trial of two dogs simultaneously, not requiring
any co-operation in quartering." In brace or
team stakes, only one brace or team is down at
a time.

Although the trial in single stakes is to be
carried on " simultaneously," you will note that
the rule does not provide whether the two dogs
are to work on the same ground, or are each to
have a separate beat. The word is used only in
contradistinction to having the dogs down one
at a time.

At the early trials of the Sporting Spaniel
Society the latter method obtained, but soon it
was perceived to be too slow and tedious ; most
of its members were anxious to adopt the
procedure of the Pointer and Setter Trials, but
one important spaniel member was opposed to
this. A non-committal wording was therefore
introduced, so that the two dogs could be run
at the discretion of the judges, either parallel or
practically on the same ground.

The procedure at the Spaniel Club trials has
followed much the same course, and although in
their case the change was slower, and the rule
now reads—" All dogs competing at the Trials
may be tried either singly or in pairs, but not on
the same ground "—the " in pairs " system has
been followed for the last five or six years.
Moreover, at last season's Trials it was no
uncommon sight to see two dogs working the

same ground—a method which admits of a direct comparison between the two dogs under identical conditions of ground and scent, and so lessens the element of luck so far as game-finding capacity is concerned.

The district meetings have followed the lead of the more important societies. At all present-day Trials it is usual to have two dogs down at a time with parallel or overlapping beats; the judges follow the handlers; the official guns take up strategic positions on the outside of the beats, to right and left; the crowd comes behind—if well ordered, some way behind—the judges; and the handlers awaiting their turn, if wise, bring up the rear.

---

## SPANIEL FIELD TRIAL MEETINGS.

International Gundog League. Sporting Spaniel Society. (H. W. Carlton, Market Harborough.) First Trials, Jan. 3rd, 1899.

Spaniel Club. (P. Lee, Wem, Salop.) First Trials, Jan. 17th, 1900.

Horsham and District Dog League. (N. Oddie, North Lodge, Horsham.) First Trials, 1903.

Northern and Midlands Spaniel Club. (A. H. Ogle, Ing Dene, Colne, Lancashire.) First Trials, 1909.

Scottish Field Trial Assoc ation. (A. M. Formby, 37, Melville Street, Edinburgh ) First Trials, 1910.

Cheshire, N. Wales, and Shropshire Society. (H. Lister Reade, Horton, Congleton, Cheshire.) First Trials, 1912.

Western Counties Spaniel Club.   (H. Scott, 27, East Street
    Taunton.)   First Trials, 1912.

Midland Counties Field Trial Society.   (H. W. Carlton,
    Market Harborough.)   First Trials, 1921.

English Springer Club.   (W. Humphrey, Wallop Hall
    Westbury, Salop.)   First Trials, 1921.

———

Championship (held in 1913 and 1921).   The Kennel Club
    (84, Piccadilly London, W.).

# INDEX.

Retrieving—
>   first lessons in, 30
>>      place for, 31
>>      object to be used,
>>          31, 36, 37
>>      taking object, 38,
>>          50
>   orders, waiting for, 22, 43
>   check-cord, 49, 87
>   Sir H. Smith's method,
>       50
>   French method, 53
>   further lessons, rabbits,
>       60
>>          woodcock, &c., 61
>   hints, 64

Rough shoots, 20, 82, 129
>   stuff, 16, 20, 65, 128

Self-control of dog, 8, 101
>   of handler, 87
Shooting to spaniel, Chapter
>   VIII.
Shot, drop to, 21, 54, 75, 85,
>   87, 89
>>          teaching, 54
"Sit," 99
Smith, Sir H., 50
Smith, E. M., 119, 122
Spaniel Club, 130
Spaniel, perfect, Chapter II.
Spoiling dog, avoid, 86, 88
Sport, breaking for, 7, 123,
>   129
Sporting Spaniel Society, 130
>       Field Trial rules, 19, 89,
>           126, 129
Standing rabbits, 18, 81

Steadiness, necessary, 20
>   foundation of, 27, 75
>   first lessons in, 42
>   in rabbit enclosure, 44
>   in field, to rabbit, 43, 75
>>          to shot, 85, 86
>   and see "Dropping."
Stopping to command, 99
Style, 14, 126

Tame rabbits, use of, 43
Thick cover, 16, 20, 65, 128
>   teaching to work, 65
Thorndike, Professor, 110,
>   114, 115, 122
Thrashing, avoid, 9
Thresh-cord. See "Check-
>   cord."
Trail, laying, 62
Turning, to whistle, 57, 69,
>   74, 127

Unsteadiness, overcoming, 87
"Up," 39
Up wind, 69, 72

Voice, avoid use of, 55, 127

"Wait," 99
Watch your dog, 12
Water, 96
Whistle, coming to, 55
>   turning to, 57, 69, 74, 127
Will power, use of, 12
Wind, up, first lessons in
>   hunting, 69, 72
>   down or cross, 78
Working    ground.    See
>   "Hunting."

"Yes," 101

PRINTED BY THE FIELD PRESS LTD., WINDSOR HOUSE,
BREAM'S BUILDINGS, LONDON, E.C. 4.

# The History of Retrievers

CHARLES C. ELEY.          *Price 10s. 6d. net.   Postage 6d.*

Incorporating a Record of Retriever Trials by Walter Baxendale, Secretary to the International Gundog League, and a chapter on the Future of Retriever Trials by Captain Harry Eley.

> *The Scottish Field :* " This is a book which retriever owners have long been waiting for, and they are thrice happy in the brilliance and practicality of Mr. Eley and his collaborators."

> *Our Dogs :* " ' The History of Retrievers '  .  .  .  should be in the hands of all owners who keep retrievers for field trial purposes or as gundogs."

---

# Retrievers and Retrieving

Lieut.-Col. W. G. ELEY.   Second Edition.   *Price 6s. net. Postage 8d.*

Chapters on Early Training ;  Work in the Field ; Observations ;  Retriever Trials ;  Kennel Management.

---

# Retrievers and How to Break Them for Sport and Field Trials

STEWART SMITH.   Third Edition.   *Price 3s. 6d. net. Postage 3d.*

The author, who writes from long experience and is well known in the field trial world, describes in a most concise manner the best methods of procedure.

> *Dog World :* " No sounder advice than that which the author gives in his chapters on the teaching of the young idea has ever been written."

---

THE FIELD PRESS LTD.,
Windsor House, Bream's Buildings, E.C. 4.

Lightning Source UK Ltd.
Milton Keynes UK
UKOW04f1101050615

252959UK00001B/70/P